Decadents, Symbolists, Anti-Decadents

Poetry of the 1890s

A series of facsimile reprints chosen and introduced by
R.K.R.THORNTON AND IAN SMALL

The book of the
Rhymers' Club
1892, 1894

Woodstock Books
Oxford and New York
1994

This edition first published 1994 by
Woodstock Books
Spelsbury House, Spelsbury, Oxford OX7 3JR
and
Woodstock Books
387 Park Avenue South
New York, NY 10016-8810

ISBN 1 85477 136 1
The 1892 volume is reproduced by permission
from a copy in Reading University Library
New matter copyright © Woodstock Books 1994
The poems by Ernest Rhys are reprinted
by permission of J.M. Dent & Sons Ltd

British Library Cataloguing-in-Publication Data
A catalogue record for this book is
available from the British Library

Library of Congress Cataloging-in-Publication Data
Rhymers' Club (London, England)
    The book of the Rhymers' Club: 1892-1894.
        p. cm. — (Decadents, symbolists, anti-decadents)
    Reprint (1st). Previously published: London: E. Mathews,
    1892.
    Reprint (2nd). Previously published: The second book of
    the Rhymers' Club. London: E. Mathews & J. Lane, 1894.
    The 1892 volume is reproduced from a copy in Reading
    University Library.
    Includes bibliographical references.
    ISBN 1-85477-136-1
    1. English poetry – 19th century.   I. Rhymers' Club
    (London, England). Second book of the Rhymers' Club.
    II. Title. III. Series.
    PR1223.R52   1993
    821'.808—dc20   93-31595
                                                     CIP

Printed and bound in Great Britain by
Smith Settle
Otley, West Yorkshire LS21 3JP

1002185175

Introduction

There are conflicting versions of the founding of the Rhymers' Club, but in H. Guy Harrison's bibliography at the end of Victor Plarr's book on Ernest Dowson (1914) we find the most authoritative account of the make-up of the club. It cites fourteen names 'from a list in the handwriting of Dr G. A. Greene, who acted as hon. secretary to a club without rules or officers.' In quoting the list, we are adding in square brackets the dates not provided in Plarr:

The Rhymers' Club consisted of the following:

John Davidson[1]	.	.	.	(1857-1909)
Ernest Dowson	.	.	.	(1867-1900)
Edwin J. Ellis	.	.	.	(18[48-1916])
George Arthur Greene	.	.	.	(1853-[1921])
Lionel Johnson	.	.	.	(1867-1902)
Arthur Cecil Hillier	.	.	.	(18[57-1914])
Richard Le Gallienne	.	.	.	(1866-[1947])
Victor Plarr	.	.	.	(1863-[1929])
Ernest Radford	.	.	.	(1857-[1919])
Ernest Rhys	.	.	.	(1859-[1946])
Thomas Wm. Rolleston	.	.	.	(1857-[1920])
Arthur Symons	.	.	.	(1865-[1945])
John Todhunter	.	.	.	(1839-[1916])
Wm. Butler Yeats	.	.	.	(1865-[1939])

1. John Davidson, though a member of the club, did not contribute to the books. Besides members, the club had at one time affiliated to itself the following permanent guests: – John Gray, Edward Rose, J. T. Nettleship, Morley Roberts, A. B. Chamberlain, Edward Garnett and William Theodore Peters.

Some of these names suggest Irish origins for the club. Nettleship and Ellis had formed a 'Brotherhood' with J. B. Yeats, the father of the poet, in the 1860s, and others, like Todhunter, Rolleston, Greene and Hillier were Trinity College Dublin men and had published in the TCD magazine *Kottabos*. The Irish members perhaps organised themselves into a club in 1890, which was re-formed with the addition of English members in the early months of 1891 into the Rhymers' Club. Or perhaps, as Ernest Rhys wrote in *Everyman remembers* (1931), 'the Rhymers' Club was set going at the Old Cheshire Cheese in Fleet Street. The three first members were T. W. Rolleston, W. B. Yeats and myself. Each of us asked other Rhymers to come to the club suppers, and we soon reached the allotted number of ten.' Yeats wrote in *Autobiographies* that he once said when the gathering was rather large, 'None of us can say who will succeed, or even who has not talent. The only thing certain about us is that we are too many.'

The club was certainly gathering together its verses in 1891 and by that time Le Gallienne and Symons had moved to London, where Dowson and Johnson were already established. For a few years, the members met in the Cheshire Cheese or in people's homes to discuss the latest poetry. The club survived long enough to publish two anthologies of poems. There were plans being made for a third, but by 1895 the members were beginning to disperse or their lives were starting to find different pressures and shapes. There were some vestiges of the club as late as 1896.

The rules for the two published books were that Rhymers were allowed to include a maximum of six and a minimum of three pieces which would be chosen from a submission of twice that number by a selection committee of four. Elkin Mathews published the first volume in a strictly limited edition in 1892 while the *Second book of the Rhymers' Club* was published under the joint imprint of Mathews and Lane in 1894, almost coinciding with the first volume of the same publishers' *The Yellow book*. Richard Le Gallienne once said that the only thing that the Rhymers had in common was a publisher, but there are distinctive 1890s themes in the two books: London or the city is a popular subject, especially in the second book; the Celtic flavour remains strong; death and its relation to life occupy several poets; and there is a consciousness of artifice. However, the presence of the Fabian and positivist Ernest Radford's mild mockery of 'The wail of the decadent' and T. W. Rolleston's 'Cycling song' with its Kiplingesque rhythm remind us that no easy generalisations can be made.

The club met for less than five years, many of its members are more or less unknown, and of its two publications only a combined total of eleven hundred copies were printed for England and America of which only nine hundred were for sale; but the club has passed into literary history as a gathering of some significance. There are three main reasons for this. First, the club had among its members poets with a wide range of contacts in the literary and reviewing world of the day, so that it was well publicised and well received by the critics. Yeats wrote in a letter of July 1891 that 'Owing to the Rhymers' Club I have a certain influence with reviewers' and he made the club the subject of one of his *Letters to the new island* in 1892, so that there was publicity in America, which necessitated the producing of a hundred and fifty copies for that market. Second, the two books gathered a number of poems of the highest quality which would be regarded as central to any idea of the 1890s. They included first or very early printings of poems like Dowson's 'Nuns of the Perpetual Adoration', *'O mors, quam amara est'*, *'Amor umbratilis'*, 'Extreme unction', 'To one in Bedlam' and *'Non sum qualis eram bonae sub regno Cynarae'*, Johnson's 'By the statue of King Charles at Charing Cross', 'The last music', 'Mystic and cavalier' and 'The dark angel', Symons's 'Javanese dancers' and 'Nora on the pavement', and Yeats's 'The man who

dreamed of fairyland', and 'The lake isle of Innisfree'.
Even Plarr's 'Epitaphium citharistriae' and Le Gallienne's
'A ballad of London' mark high moments in their
authors' work and contain essentially 1890s
characteristics. Third, the club was made the focus of
mythologies of the period, particularly by Yeats. His
prose account of the formative influences of his early
manhood in *Autobiographies* makes his fellow Rhymers
into 'The Tragic Generation' of *poètes maudits* tragically
cut off at an early age because of their fated devotion to
an artistic ideal. This view seems a little ungrounded
when one looks at the fact that only four of Greene's list
of fourteen Rhymers failed to reach the age of sixty, and
three lived to over eighty. But, as always, Yeats's version
has power and influence, especially when reinforced in
his poetry, centring on Dowson and Johnson. In his
account of the Rhymers in 'The Grey Rock' Yeats
describes the

> Poets with whom I learned my trade,
> Companions of the Cheshire Cheese,

and sets up images of the Rhymers as permanent
guardians of the aesthetic ideal, sacrificing all to their art.
It is Yeats's picture that remains with us when we think of
the Rhymers' Club:

> Since, tavern comrades, you have died,
> Maybe your images have stood,
> Mere bone and muscle thrown aside,
> Before that roomful or as good.
> You had to face your ends when young –
> 'Twas wine or women, or some curse –
> But never made a poorer song
> That you might have a heavier purse,
> Nor gave loud service to a cause
> That you might have a troop of friends.

You kept the Muses' sterner laws;
And unrepenting faced your ends,
And therefore earned the right – and yet
Dowson and Johnson most I praise –
To troop with those the world's forgot,
And copy their proud steady gaze.

R.K.R.T.
I.S.

Select Bibliography

This list is selective, concentrating on poetry from the decade of the 1890s for the better-known authors while being more inclusive for the lesser-known authors. For those marked with an asterisk, fuller bibliographies can be found in other titles in this series.

John Davidson*
In a music-hall and other poems, 1891.
Fleet Street eclogues, 1893.
Ballads and songs, 1894.
A second series of Fleet Street eclogues, 1896.
New ballads, 1897.
The last ballad and other poems, 1899.
See also *The poems of John Davidson*, ed. Andrew Turnbull, 2 vols, 1973.

Ernest Dowson*
Verses, 1896.
Decorations, 1899.
See also *The poetical works of Ernest Dowson*, ed. Desmond Flower, 1934, 1950 and 1967.

Edwin J. Ellis
Doda's birthday, 1873.
When is your birthday?, 1883.
Fate in Arcadia and other poems, 1892.
Seen in three days, 1893.
The works of William Blake, ed. with W. B. Yeats, 1893.
The man of seven offers (novel), 1895.
Sancan the bard (verse drama), 1895.
Anthony Polgate (novel), 1904.

George A. Greene
Italian lyrists of to-day (translation), 1893.
Dantesques, 1903.
Songs of the open air, 1912.

Arthur Cecil Hillier

The history of modern painting by Richard Müther
(translation with G. A. Greene and Ernest Dowson),
3 vols, 1895-6.

Lionel Johnson*

Poems, 1895.
Ireland with other poems, 1897.
See also *The complete poems of Lionel Johnson*, ed. Iain
Fletcher, 1953 (second and revised edition, New York,
1982).

Richard Le Gallienne*

English poems, 1892.
Robert Louis Stevenson and other poems, 1895.
Rubáiyát of Omar Khayyám, 1897.
See *The quest of the golden boy* by Geoffrey Smerdon and
Richard Whittington-Egan, 1960.

Victor Plarr*

In the Dorian mood, 1896.
The tragedy of Asgard, 1905.
See *Collected poems of Victor Plarr*, ed. Iain Fletcher, 1974.

Ernest Radford

Translations from Heine and other verses, Cambridge, 1882.
Measured steps, 1884.
Songs in the whirlwind, with Ada Radford, 1886.
Chambers twain, 1890.
Old and new, 1895.
A collection of poems, 1906.

Ernest Rhys

A London rose and other poems, 1894.
Welsh ballads and other poems, 1898.
The whistling maid, 1900.
Lays of the Round Table, 1905.
The leaf burners, 1918.
Rhymes for everyman, 1933.

Songs of the sun, 1937.
See *Everyman remembers,* 1931.

T. W. Rolleston
A life of Lessing, 1889.
A discourse upon Walt Whitman, 1883.
Deirdre, 1897.
Sea spray. Verses and translations, 1909.
The high deeds of Finn, 1910.
See *Portrait of an Irishman,* by Charles H. Rolleston, 1939,
    and *Whitman and Rolleston, a correspondence,* Indiana,
    1951.

Arthur Symons*
Days and nights, 1889.
Silhouettes, 1892.
London nights, 1895.
Amoris Victima, 1897.
Images of good and evil, 1899.

John Todhunter
Laurella and other poems, 1876.
Alcestis: a dramatic poem, 1879.
Forest songs, 1881.
The banshee and other poems, 1888.
A Sicilian idyll (pastoral verse play), 1890.
The black cat. A play in three acts, 1895.
Sounds and sweet airs, 1905.
See *Selected poems,* ed. D. L. Todhunter and A. P. Graves,
    1929 and *Irish book lover,* December and January 1916-17.

W. B. Yeats*
The Countess Kathleen and various legends and lyrics, 1892.
Poems, 1895.
The wind among the reeds, 1899.
See *The variorum edition of the poems of W. B. Yeats,* ed. Peter
    Allt and Russell K. Alspach, New York, 1957, and
    Collected poems, 1950.

Useful works to consult

W. B. Yeats, 'The Rhymers' Club' in *Letters to the new island*, Cambridge, Mass, 1934.

W. B. Yeats, *Autobiographies*, 1955.

Karl Beckson, 'New dates for the Rhymers' Club' in *English literature in transition*, 13 1 (1970), 37-38.

R. K. R. Thornton, 'Dates for the Rhymers' Club' in *English literature in transition*, 14 1 (1971), 49-53.

Karl Beckson, 'Yeats and the Rhymers' Club' in *Yeats studies* 1 (1971), 20-41.

Norman Alford, *The Rhymers' Club: poets of the tragic generation*, Victoria, BC, 1981.

Joann Gardner, *Yeats and the Rhymers' Club: a nineties' perspective*, New York, 1989.

THE BOOK

OF

THE RHYMERS' CLUB

THE BOOK

OF THE

RHYMERS' CLUB

LONDON
ELKIN MATHEWS
AT THE SIGN OF THE BODLEY HEAD
IN VIGO STREET
1892

J. MILLER AND SON, PRINTERS, EDINBURGH

THE RHYMERS' CLUB

—✳—

ERNEST DOWSON

EDWIN J. ELLIS

G. A. GREENE

LIONEL JOHNSON

RICHARD LE GALLIENNE

VICTOR PLARR

ERNEST RADFORD

ERNEST RHYS

T. W. ROLLESTON

ARTHUR SYMONS

JOHN TODHUNTER

W. B. YEATS

A FEW of the following poems have been published in various periodicals, such as the *The National Observer*, *The Academy*, *Macmillan*, *The Century*, *Black and White*, etc., to the Editors of which we return thanks for courteous permission to republish them.

CONTENTS

		PAGE
At the Rhymers' Club : The Toast, .	*Ernest Rhys* . .	1
What of the Darkness ? . . .	*Richard Le Gallienne*	3
By the Statue of King Charles the First at Charing Cross, . .	*Lionel Johnson* . .	4
A Man who dreamed of Fairyland, .	*W. B. Yeats* . .	7
Carmelite Nuns of the Perpetual Adoration, ...	*Ernest Dowson* . .	10
Love and Death (*Æsop's Fable*), .	*Ernest Radford* .	12
Epitaphium Citharistriæ, . . .	*Victor Plarr* . .	15
Beatrice's Song (*From 'The Poison Flower'*), ...	*John Todhunter* .	16
The Pathfinder, ...	*G. A. Greene* . .	18
The Broken Tryst, ...	*Arthur Symons* . .	19
New Words and Old, . . .	*Edwin J. Ellis* . .	21
A Ring's Secret, ...	*T. W. Rolleston* .	24
The Wedding of Pale Bronwen, .	*Ernest Rhys* . .	25

		PAGE
Beauty Accurst, ...	*Richard Le Gallienne*	28
O Mors! quam amara est memoria tua homini pacem habenti in substantiis suis!	*Ernest Dowson* . .	30
The Sonnet, ...	*G. A. Greene* . .	32
A Burden of Easter Vigil, . .	*Lionel Johnson* . .	33
To One Beloved, . . .	*John Todhunter* . .	34
Music and Memory, . . .	*Arthur Symons* . .	35
In a Norman Church, . .	*Victor Plarr* . .	36
Father Gilligan, . . .	*W. B. Yeats* . .	38
Amor Umbratilis, . . .	*Ernest Dowson* . .	41
At the Hearth, ...	*Edwin J. Ellis* . .	42
Keats' Grave, ...	*G. A. Greene* . .	43
On Marlowe, ...	*Ernest Rhys* . .	44
At Citoyenne Tussaud's, . .	*Victor Plarr* . .	45
Ballade of the 'Cheshire Cheese,'.	*T. W. Rolleston* .	46
The Last Music, . . .	*Lionel Johnson* . .	48
A Death in the Forest, . .	*Arthur Symons* . .	50
'Onli Deathe' . . .	*Ernest Radford* . .	52
Ad Domnulam Suam, . .	*Ernest Dowson* . .	53
Dedication of ' Irish Tales,' .	*W. B. Yeats* . .	54
Quatrain (The Epitaph on Hafiz, a young Linnet), . . .	*Ernest Rhys* . .	56
Javanese Dancers : a Silhouette,	*Arthur Symons* . .	57
Chorus from 'Iphigeneia in Aulis'	*John Todhunter* . .	58
To a Greek Gem, . . .	*Victor Plarr* . .	61
Arts Lough, ...	*G. A. Greene* . .	62
In Falmouth Harbour, . .	*Lionel Johnson* . .	63

		PAGE
A Choice of Likenesses,	*Ernest Radford*	66
To Autumn,	*Richard Le Gallienne*	67
Vanitas,	*Ernest Dowson* .	69
A Fairy Song,	*W. B. Yeats* .	71
Mothers of Men,	*Edwin J. Ellis* .	72
Chatterton in Holborn,	*Ernest Rhys*	75
To a Passionist,	*Lionel Johnson* .	78
Freedom in a Suburb,	*Ernest Radford*	80
Quatrain : Les Bourgeoises,	*Ernest Rhys* .	81
Drifting,	*G. A. Greene* .	82
Villanelle of Sunset, .	*Ernest Dowson* .	83
The Lake Isle of Innisfree,	*W. B. Yeats* .	84
A Sundial : Flowers of Time,	*Ernest Radford*	85
Twilight-Piece,	*Victor Plarr* .	86
Sunset in the City. .	*Richard Le Gallienne*	87
An Epitaph,	*W. B. Yeats* .	88
Proverbs, .	*Edwin J. Ellis* .	89
Plato in London,	*Lionel Johnson* .	90
The Song of the Songsmiths,	*G. A. Greene* .	92

AT THE RHYMERS' CLUB

———

THE TOAST

Set fools unto their folly!
    Our folly is pure wit,
As 'twere the Muse turned jolly:
For poets' melancholy,—
    We will not think of it.

As once Rare Ben and Herrick
    Set older Fleet Street mad,
With wit not esoteric,
And laughter that was lyric,
    And roystering rhymes and glad:

As they, we drink defiance
    To-night to all but Rhyme,
And most of all to Science,
And all such skins of lions
    That hide the ass of time.

A

To-night, to rhyme as they did
  Were well,—ah, were it ours,
Who find the Muse degraded,
And changed, I fear, and faded,
  Her laurel crown and flowers.

Ah rhymers, for that sorrow
  The more o'ertakes delight,
The more this madness borrow:—
If care be king to-morrow,
  To toast Queen Rhyme to-night.

ERNEST RHYS.

WHAT OF THE DARKNESS?

(To the Happy Dead People)

WHAT of the Darkness? Is it very fair?
Are there great calms and find ye silence there?
Like soft-shut lilies all your faces glow
With some strange peace our faces never know,
With some great faith our faces never dare.
Dwells it in Darkness? Do ye find it there?

Is it a Bosom where tired heads may lie?
Is it a Mouth to kiss our weeping dry?
Is it a Hand to still the pulse's leap?
Is it a Voice that holds the runes of sleep?
Day shows us not such comfort anywhere.
Dwells it in Darkness? Do ye find it there?

Out of the day's deceiving light we call,
Day that shows man so great and God so small,
That hides the stars and magnifies the grass;
O! is the Darkness too a lying glass,
Or undistracted do ye find Truth there?—
What of the Darkness? Is it very fair?

RICHARD LE GALLIENNE.

BY THE STATUE OF KING CHARLES
THE FIRST AT CHARING CROSS

SOMBRE and rich, the skies;
Great glooms, and starry plains.
Gently the night wind sighs;
Else a vast silence reigns.

The splendid silence clings
Around me : and around
The saddest of all kings
Crowned, and again discrowned.

Comely and calm, he rides
Hard by his own Whitehall :
Only the night wind glides :
No crowds, nor rebels, brawl.

Gone, too, his Court : and yet,
The stars his courtiers are :
Stars in their stations set;
And every wandering star.

Alone he rides, alone,
The fair and fatal king:
Dark night is all his own,
That strange and solemn thing.

Which are more full of fate :
The stars : or those sad eyes ?
Which are more still and great :
Those brows : or the dark skies ?

Although his whole heart yearn
In passionate tragedy :
Never was face so stern
With sweet austerity.

Vanquished in life, his death
By beauty made amends :
The passing of his breath
Won his defeated ends.

Brief life, and hapless ? Nay :
Through death, life grew sublime.
Speak after sentence ? Yea :
And to the end of time.

Armoured he rides, his head
Bare to the stars of doom :
He triumphs now, the dead,
Beholding London's gloom.

Our wearier spirit faints,
Vexed in the world's employ :
His soul was of the Saints;
And art to him was joy.

King, tried in fires of woe !
Men hunger for thy grace :
And through the night I go,
Loving thy mournful face.

Yet, when the city sleeps;
When all the cries are still :
The stars and heavenly deeps
Work out their perfect will.

LIONEL JOHNSON.

A MAN WHO DREAMED OF FAIRYLAND

I

HE stood among a crowd at Drumahair,
   His heart hung all upon a silken dress,
   And he had known at last some tenderness
Before earth made of him her sleepy care;
But when a man poured fish into a pile,
   It seemed they raised their little silver heads
   And sang how day a Druid twilight sheds
Upon a dim, green, well-beloved isle,
Where people love beside star-laden seas;
   How Time may never mar their fairy vows
   Under the woven roofs of quicken boughs ;—
The singing shook him out of his new ease.

II

As he went by the sands of Lisadill
   His mind ran all on money cares and fears,
   And he had known at last some prudent years
Before they heaped his grave under the hill;

But while he passed before a plashy place,
 A lug-worm with its gray and muddy mouth
 Sang how somewhere to north or east or south
There dwelt a gay, exulting, gentle race;
And how beneath those three times blessed skies
 A Danaan fruitage makes a shower of moons
 And as it falls awakens leafy tunes;—
And at that singing he was no more wise.

III

He mused beside the well of Scanavin,
 He mused upon his mockers. Without fail
 His sudden vengeance were a country tale
Now that deep earth has drunk his body in;
But one small knot-grass growing by the rim
 Told where—ah, little, all-unneeded voice!—
 Old Silence bids a lonely folk rejoice,
And chaplet their calm brows with leafage dim
And how, when fades the sea-strewn rose of day,
 A gentle feeling wraps them like a fleece,
 And all their trouble dies into its peace;—
The tale drove his fine angry mood away.

IV

He slept under the hill of Lugnagall,
 And might have known at last unhaunted sleep
 Under that cold and vapour-turbaned steep,

Now that old earth had taken man and all:
Were not the worms that spired about his bones
  A-telling with their low and reedy cry
  Of how God leans His hands out of the sky,
To bless that isle with honey in His tones.
That none may feel the power of squall and wave,
  And no one any leaf-crowned dances miss
  Until He burn up Nature with a kiss;—
The man has found no comfort in the grave.

                      W. B. YEATS.

CARMELITE NUNS OF THE PERPETUAL ADORATION

Calm, sad, secure; behind high convent walls;
  These watch the sacred lamp, these watch and pray:
And it is one with them, when evening falls;
  And one with them, the cold return of day.

These heed not time: their nights and days they make
  Into a long, returning rosary;
Whereon their lives are threaded for Christ's sake:
  Meekness and vigilance and chastity.

A vowed patrol, in silent companies,
  Life long they keep before the living Christ:
In the dim church, their prayers and penances,
  Are fragrant incense to the Sacrificed.

Outside, the world is wild and passionate;
  Man's weary laughter, and his sick despair
Entreat at their impenetrable gate:
  They heed no voices in their dream of prayer.

They saw the glory of the world displayed,
　　They saw the bitter of it, and the sweet :
They knew the roses of the world should fade,
　　And be trod under by the hurrying feet.

Therefore they rather put away desire,
　　And crossed their hands and came to Sanctuary;
And veiled their heads and put on coarse attire :
　　Because their comeliness was vanity.

And there they rest; they have serene insight
　　Of the illuminating dawn to be :
Mary's sweet Star dispels for them the night,
　　The proper darkness of humanity.

Calm, sad, serene; with faces worn and mild :
　　Surely their choice of vigil is the best ?
Yea! for our roses fade, the world is wild;
　　But there, beside the altar, there, is rest.

ERNEST DOWSON.

LOVE AND DEATH

(Æsop's Fable)

LOVE, on a summer day,
    Faint with heat,
    Tired with play,
Came to a grotto fair,
And courted slumber there,
And flung his darts away.

This was, the Fable saith,
The very cave of Death;
But this Love did not know:
As he had sped a shaft
With more than common craft,
Once—in his sleep—he laughed:
At dawn he rose to go.

Love was at parting fain
  To have his darts again:—
' O Love, beware, beware !
  The shafts of Death are there,

Of mortal man the bane !'
But Love cared not a stiver:
Intent on human hearts
He gathered to his quiver
His own with Death's black darts;
And glorious in the morning
He winged his golden way,
Sweet maidens had forewarning
That Love was on the way,
Strong men all labour scorning,
Did nothing on that day,
For dallying with a maiden
Is neither work nor play.
Old men and women saddened
In the dragging of the years,
On a sudden gladdened
To laughter and to tears.
Love was on earth again,
Intending ill to none.
(He wotted not of pain
Blind creature of the Sun !)
He knew not what he did,
Nor rested till 'twas done,
But old and young
He rushed amid,
And shot his arrows
Everyone.

And some cried out—' Ah, Death he deals !
And surely Death did come,
And others cried—' 'tis Love, 'tis Love !'
And Love there was for some.

ERNEST RADFORD.

EPITAPHIUM CITHARISTRIAE

STAND not uttering sedately
   Trite oblivious praise above her !
Rather say you saw her lately
   Lightly kissing her last lover.

Whisper not, 'There is a reason
   Why we bring her no white blossom.'
Since the snowy bloom's in season
   Strow it on her sleeping bosom !

Oh, for it would be a pity
   To o'erpraise her or to flout her.
She was wild, and sweet, and witty—
   Let's not say dull things about her.

               VICTOR PLARR.

BEATRICE'S SONG

From ' The Poison Flower '

A chamber with a window overlooking RAPPACCINI'S *garden.*
GUASCONTI *alone.* BEATRICE *sings in the garden.*

SONG

Heap me a mound of holy spice,
With camphor, sandal, cinnamon,
Gums and rich balms, like that whereon
The magian phœnix burns and dies!
There let pale women hush their cries
To do in desolate array
Soft rites, and chant low litanies,
Till thunders roll around the skirts of day:
Then fling the torch and come away,
Come away, and leave the kindled pyre
Where Love lies dead, that was the world's desire!

[GUASCONTI *listens intently, then runs to the window, looks out*
and draws back disappointed.]

GUAS. Earth has her siren : all my senses sing,
And the lone caverns of my inward ear

Sound on, like musing shells that lull themselves
To sad content, with ocean's lingering boom.
O rich remembrancer of worlds unknown
For which I am long homesick, sing once more!
(He draws a chair to the window and sits)

BEATRICE'S *Song (further off)*

The aloe feels the year of years,
Wakes, and the wandering bees it calls—

(The song ends abruptly, he looks out again)

GUAS. I knew I should see nothing; save the glow
Of noon o'er that dread garden, where methinks
Each venomous thing sprouts rankly as the weeds
Upon forgotten graves. In the deep hush
No cricket's tune is heard, only the stir
Of some quick-darting lizard. Sleeping snakes
Bask on hot stones, coiled furies, in the sun,
Enough to furnish cold Medusa's hair;
And snake-like plants, nameless in mortal tongue,
Pant from their gorgeous flowers, drinking the blaze,
Subtle intoxication. I grow faint
With the sweet horror. O that song! That song
Voluptuous Lilith sang o'er Adam's sleep,
And flushed his blood with sensuous sorcery!

JOHN TODHUNTER.

B

THE PATHFINDER

FULL of world-weariness, and of the sense
  Of unachievement, lies the toiler down
  Who hath made smooth the way, but sees the crown
Fade in the sunset far through depths immense

Of unassaulted heaven: vain vision, hence!
  Yet soon again amid the shadows brown
  He striveth on who reacheth not: renown
Was not his aim: he hath his recompense.

Because to aspire is better than to attain:
  Because the will is nobler than the deed,
  The blossom glorious more than is the fruit;

The worker knows he hath not striven in vain;
  They shall arrive with winged and arrowy speed
  Who follow far his solitary foot.

G. A. GREENE.

THE BROKEN TRYST

THAT day a fire was in my blood;
  I could have sung : joy wrapt me round;
The men I met seemed all so good,
  I scarcely knew I trod the ground.

How easy seemed all toil ! I laughed
  To think that once I hated it.
The sunlight thrilled like wine, I quaffed
  Delight divine and infinite.

The very day was not too long;
  I felt so patient ; I could wait,
Being certain. So, the hours in song
  Chimed out the minutes of my fate.

For she was coming, she, at last,
  I knew: I knew that bolts and bars
Could stay her not; my heart throbbed fast,
  I was not more certain of the stars.

The twilight came, grew deeper; now
  The hour struck, minutes passed, and still
The passionate fervour of her vow
  Rang in my heart's ear audible.

I had no doubt at all: I knew
  That she would come, and I was then
Most certain, while the minutes flew:
  Ah, how I scorned all other men!

Next moment! Ah! it was—was not!
  I heard the stillness of the street.
Night came. The stars had not forgot.
  The moonlight fell about my feet.

So I rebuked my heart, and said:
  'Be still, for she is coming, see,
Next moment—coming. Ah, her tread,
  I hear it coming—it is she!'

And then a woman passed. The hour
  Rang heavily along the air.
I had no hope, I had no power
  To think—for thought was but despair.

A thing had happened. What? My brain
  Dared not so much as guess the thing.
And yet the sun would rise again
  Next morning! I stood marvelling.

ARTHUR SYMONS.

NEW WORDS AND OLD

I

'In the same day thou eatest thou shalt die.'
    Oh long, short day, even now we see appear
    Thy sunrise hope, thy chill of evening fear
When the reproving Voice comes wandering by.
Thou hast done well to take eternity
    From this false world of ours, but leave it near.
    The little door of death is always here;
Thou openest our cage that we may fly.
    Some perfect things thou leavest, the white life
Of the heavy lily in the month of June
Thou hast not sullied, nor the wood-bird's tune,
    Nor the boy's dream that he shall find for wife
So sweet a maid that even in love's high noon
    Pure prayer shall stay his kisses' purer strife.

II

Unfearing, like a new-caught lion wild
    Who treads despair and meets the triumphant
        crowd,
    So Adam came, when the voice called aloud.
Then God, his image still but half defiled

Saw darkening in the face of his own child,
  Whom wisdom had made modest, but not bow'd,
  Who, hating death, forgot not to be proud,
Who sinned from love, and sought no mercy mild.
  'Who told thee thou wert naked?' Ah: who told?
'Who told me that this woman at my side,
  Whom thou hast given, and made so tender-eyed,
  Was less forgiveable to Justice Old
Than unto me, but yesterday untried?'
  But Christ has died, and man is no more bold.

III

The Rose and Lily by the golden Gate
  Of Heaven's own garden, where the trailing dress
  Of the sweet virgin, followed by a press
Of angels among angels fortunate,
Being the guard of her, immaculate,
  Had now but passed and left a sacredness
  Like perfume in the air that God shall bless,—
The Rose and Lily gently, without hate,
  Disputed which should be the flower of choice.
'For being white as I,' the Lily cried,
  'Mary was chosen.'   Then with tenderer voice,
'But loved for being like me,' the Rose replied.
  Returning, Mary laid upon her breast
  Both flowers, and none could answer which was
    best.

IV

So it were strange if I should close my eyes
        And fear to find God's mercy on the shore,
        Did I this night pass on for evermore
Beyond the level rays of the sunrise.
I come not with a claim for Paradise;
        Yet though I shook the Tree of Evil sore,
        And though the fruit I tasted to the core,
To go unto the Father I will arise.
        Shall He that bade us to forgive, but now,
The trespasser, though trespass brought dismay
        And poverty, and pain, e'er He allow
That entrance to forgiveness we might pray,—
Shall God—That is not hurt—still turn away?
        I am unworthy, Father, but not Thou.

EDWIN J. ELLIS.

A RING'S SECRET

CAN you forgive me, that I wear,
Dearest, a curl of sunny hair
Not yours, yet for the sake of love
And plighted troth it minds me of?
'Tis in this quaint old signet ring,
A curious, chased engraven thing
I bought because it charm'd my eye
And told of the last century.
Pure gold it was, but dull and blotched,
And brightening it one day I touch'd
A spring that ope'd a little lid,
And there, for generations hid
In its small shrine of pallid gold
—They made such toys in days of old—
A shred of golden hair lay curled;
Worth all the gold of all the world
To some one once, who now—Heigh ho,
That was a hundred years ago!

But dearest, if he loved as I,
He loved unto eternity.

T. W. ROLLESTON.

THE WEDDING OF PALE BRONWEN

I

THE wind was waked by the morning light,
　And it cried in the gray birch-tree,
And the cry was plain in Bronwen's bower,
　' Oh, Bronwen, come to me ! '

Pale, pale sleeps Bronwen, pale she wakes,
　'What bird to my bower is flown?'
For my lover, Red Ithel, is at the wars
　Before Jerusalem town.'

But still the wind sang in the tree,
　' Come forth, 'tis your wedding morn,
And you must be wed in Holy Land
　Ere your little babe is born.'

And still the wind had her true-love's cry,
　' Kind Bronwen, come!' until
She could not rest, and rose to look
　To the sea beyond Morva Hill.

And afar came the cry over Morva Hill,
  'Kind Bronwen, come to me!'
Till she could not stay, for very love,
  And stole away to the sea.

She crossed the hill to the fishing-boats,
  And away she sailed so fine,
'Is it far, my love, in the summer sun
  To the shores of fair Palestine?'

II

There was no sun at sea that day,
  To watch pale Bronwen drown,
But the sun was hot on the deadly sands
  Before Jerusalem town.

All day Red Ithel lay dying there,
  But he thought of the far-off sea;
And he cried all day till his lips grew white,
  'Kind Bronwen, come to me!'

And so it passed till the evening time,
  And then the sea-wind came,
And he thought he lay on Morva Hill
  And heard her call his name.

He heard her voice, he held her hand,
  'This is the day,' she said,

' And this is the hour that Holy Church
    Has given for us to wed.'

  There was no strength in him to speak,
      But his eyes had yet their say,
' Kind Bronwen, now we will be wed
      Forever and ever and aye !'

III

  Beneath the sea pale Bronwen lies,
      Red Ithel beneath the sand;
  But they are one in Holy Church,
      One in love's Holy Land.

  Red Ithel lies by Jerusalem town,
      And she in the deep sea lies;
  But I trow their little babe was born
      In the gardens of Paradise.

                              ERNEST RHYS.

BEAUTY ACCURST

I AM so fair that wheresoe'er I wend
    Men yearn with strange desire to kiss my face,
Stretch out their hands to touch me as I pass,
    And women follow me from place to place.

A poet writing honey of his dear
    Leaves the wet page,—ah, leaves it long to dry,
The bride forgets it is her marriage morn,
    The bridegroom too forgets as I go by.

Within the street where my strange feet shall stray
    All markets hush and traffickers forget,
In my gold head forget their meaner gold,
    The poor man grows unmindful of his debt.

Two lovers kissing in a secret place,
    Should I draw nigh, will never kiss again;
I come between the king and his desire,
    And where I am all loving else is vain.

Lo! as I walk along the woodland way
   Strange creatures leer at me with uncouth love,
And from the grass reach upward to my breast,
   And to my mouth lean from the boughs above.

The sleepy kine move round me in desire
   And press their oozy lips upon my hair,
Toads kiss my feet and creatures of the mire,
   The snails will leave their shells to watch me there.

But all this worship—what is it to me?
   I smite the ox and crush the toad in death,
I only know I am so very fair
   And that the world was made to give me breath.

I only wait the hour when God shall rise
   Up from the star where he so long hath sat,
And bow before the wonder of my eyes,
   And set *me* there—I am so fair as that.

                  RICHARD LE GALLIENNE.

O MORS! QUAM AMARA EST MEMORIA TUA HOMINI PACEM HABENTI IN SUBSTANTIIS SUIS!

EXCEEDING sorrow
    Consumeth my sad heart !
Because to-morrow,
    We must depart,
Now is exceeding sorrow
    All my part !

Give over playing :
    Cast thy viol away:
Merely laying
    Thy head my way :
Prithee ! give over playing,
    Grave or gay.

Be no word spoken :
    Weep nothing; let a pale
Silence, unbroken
    Silence prevail :
Prithee ! be no word spoken,
    Lest I fail.

Forget to-morrow,
    Weep nothing : merely lay,
For silent sorrow,
    Thine head my way ;
Let us forget to-morrow,
    This last day !

ERNEST DOWSON.

THE SONNET

I HEAR the quatrains' rolling melody,
  The second answering back her sister's sounds
  Like a repeated music, that resounds
A second time with varying harmony:

Then come the tercets with full-voiced reply,
  And close the solemn strain in sacred bounds,
  While all the time one growing thought expounds
One palpitating passion's ecstasy.

Ah! could I hear thy thoughts so answer mine
  As quatrain echoes quatrain, soft and low,
  Two hearts in rhyme and time one golden glow;

If so two lives one music might entwine,
  What melody of life were mine and thine,
  Till song-like comes the ending all must know!

G. A. GREENE.

A BURDEN OF EASTER VIGIL

A WHILE meet Doubt and Faith :
For either sigheth, and saith;
  That He is dead
To-day: the linen cloths cover His head,
That hath at last, whereon to rest; a rocky bed.

  Come ! for the pangs are done,
  That overcast the sun,
   So bright to-day !
And moved the Roman soldier : come away !
Hath sorrow more to weep? hath pity more to say?

  Why wilt thou linger yet ?
  Think on dark Olivet;
   On Calvary Stem :
Think, from the happy birth at Bethlehem,
To this last woe and passion at Jerusalem !

  This only can be said :
  He loved us all; is dead;
   May rise again.
But if He rise not?   Over the far main,
The sun of glory falls indeed: the stars are plain.

LIONEL JOHNSON.

C

TO ONE BELOVED

AWAY from thee, my love!   Away from thee?
O, in the soul of sense, never more near,
Thy love broods in the genial glow of day,
Thy tender solace fills the hush of night!

All hopes or fears, all triumph or defeat,
All shy vicissitudes the spirit knows,
Seem but the changes of that shadowy clime
Where Love doth bless thee from the spells of change.

All moving tales, all beauty, all delight,
Earth's multitudinous music or the sea's,
All sweet and shuddering chords from Life's rich lute
Set my lone pulses murmuring unto thee:

Murmuring in murmurs, neither passionate words,
Nor music wafting them on wings of might,
Nor seraph silence with her golden tongue,
Can ever all remurmur to thy heart.

JOHN TODHUNTER.

MUSIC AND MEMORY

(To K. W.)

Across the tides of music, in the night,
Her magical face,
A light upon it as the happy light
Of dreams in some delicious place
Under the moonlight in the night.

Music, soft throbbing music in the night,
Her memory swims
Into the brain, a carol of delight;
The cup of music overbrims
With wine of memory, in the night.

Her face across the music, in the night,
Her face a refrain,
A light that sings along the waves of light,
A memory that returns again,
Music in music, in the night.

                                    ARTHUR SYMONS.

IN A NORMAN CHURCH

As over incense-laden air
　　Stole winter twilight, soft and dim,
The folk arose from their last prayer—
　　When hark ! the children's hymn.

Round yon great pillar, circlewise,
　　The singers stand up two and two—
Small lint-haired girls from whose young eyes
　　The gray sea looks at you.

Now heavenward the pure music wins
　　With cadence soft and silvery beat.
In flutes and subtle violins
　　Are harmonies less sweet.

It is a chant with plaintive ring,
　　And rhymes and refrains old and quaint.
'Oh Monseigneur Saint Jacques,' they sing,
　　And 'Oh Assisi's Saint.'

Through deepening dusk one just can see
    The little white-capped heads that move
In time to lines turned rhythmically
    And starred with names of love.

Bred in no gentle silken ease,
    Trained to expect no splendid fate,
They are but peasant children these,
    Of very mean estate.

Nay, is that true?   To-night perhaps
    Unworldlier eyes had well discerned
Among those little gleaming caps
    An aureole that burned.

For once 'twas thought the Gates of Pearl
    Best opened to the poor that trod
The path of the meek peasant girl
    Who bore the Son of God.

VICTOR PLARR.

FATHER GILLIGAN

(A legend told by the people of Castleisland, Kerry)

THE old priest Peter Gilligan
    Was weary night and day,
For half his flock were in their beds
    Or under green sods lay.

Once while he nodded on a chair,
    At the moth-hour of eve,
Another poor man sent for him,
    And he began to grieve.

'I have no rest, nor joy, nor peace,
    For people die and die;'
And after cried he, 'God forgive!
    My body spake, not I!'

And then, half-lying on the chair,
    He knelt, prayed, fell asleep;
And the moth-hour went from the fields,
    And stars began to peep.

They slowly into millions grew,
   And leaves shook in the wind ;
And God covered the world with shade,
   And whispered to mankind.

Upon the time of sparrow chirp,
   When the moths came once more,
The old priest Peter Gilligan
   Stood upright on the floor.

'Ochone, ochone ! the man has died,
   While I slept on the chair ';
He roused his horse out of its sleep,
   And rode with little care.

He rode now as he never rode,
   By rocky lane and fen ;
The sick man's wife opened the door:
   ' Father ! you come again ! '

'And is the poor man dead ? ' he cried.
   ' He died an hour ago.'
The old priest Peter Gilligan
   In grief swayed to and fro.

' When you were gone he turned and died,
   As merry as a bird.'
The old priest Peter Gilligan
   He knelt him at that word.

'He who hath made the night of stars
  For souls who tire and bleed
Sent one of His great angels down
  To help me in my need.

'He who is wrapped in purple robes,
  With planets in his care,
Had pity on the least of things
  Asleep upon a chair.'

                              W. B. YEATS.

AMOR UMBRATILIS

A GIFT of silence, Sweet !
    Who may not ever hear :
To lay down at your unobservant feet,
    Is all the gift I bear.

I have no songs to sing,
    That you should heed or know :
I have no lilies, in full hands, to fling,
    Across the path you go.

I cast my flowers away,
    Blossoms unmeet for you :
The garland, I have gathered, in my day ;
    My rose-mary and rue.

I watch you pass and pass,
    Serene and cold : I lay
My lips upon your trodden, daisied grass,
    And turn my life away.

Yea, for I cast you, Sweet !
    This one gift, you shall take :
Like ointment, on your unobservant feet,
    My silence, for your sake.

                       ERNEST DOWSON.

AT THE HEARTH

THE kettle sang beside the bars
  A tender ballad soft and low;
Time came down from the far-off stars
  And warmed his feet before the glow.

Then Love drew near the further side,—
  Between the two, my bride and I,—
And silent I, and still my bride,
  And Love, lest Time should rouse and fly.

We might have lingered there till doom,
  If doom could come with Time asleep;
But Pity crept into the room,
  Saying, oh Time, thy children weep.

Then Time rose up and took his scythe;
  The frightened kettle ceased to sing;
But Pity, through her tears, grew blythe,
  And led him forth and kissed his wing.

EDWIN J. ELLIS.

KEATS' GRAVE

(Written when it was proposed to make a high-road over it)

Dust unto dust?   Ye are the dust of Time,
    Immortals, whose mortality is o'er;
     Names writ in water once—now evermore
Carved on remembering hearts in gold of rhyme.

What though above your heads the pantomime
    Of vulgar traffic clash with daily roar?
     'Tis the same load in life your spirits bore,
The world's indifference to souls sublime.

So all mankind moves on with ceaseless tread,
    Tho' the far goal yon mystic shadow bars,
     Along a road whose dust is heroes' lives.

Sacred no less the soil, than overhead
    That highway to whose end no sight arrives,
     A riven road ablaze with dust of stars.

                  G. A. GREENE.

ON MARLOWE *

WITH wine and blood and reckless harlotry
He sped the heroic flame of English verse;
Bethink ye, Rhymers, what your claim may be,
Who in smug suburbs put the Muse to nurse?

ERNEST RHYS.

* The Rhymers held a 'Marlowe' night, and the writer having brought no rhyme of celebration, was punished by a command to produce one on the spot, in the writing which he took a friendly revenge!

AT CITOYENNE TUSSAUD'S

THE place is full of whispers—'Mark you, sirs,
This one is he who struck our moralists mute
Before the crime which proved him wholly brute!
Mark well his face!' The gaping sight-seers
Nudge one another, and no tongue but stirs
In awe-struck comment on hat, coat and boot
Mean smirking smile, base air of smug repute,
Worn by some prince of viler murderers!

Nay, I like most these lank-tressed doctrinaires
Who cluster round their powerless guillotine,
Aquiline, delicate, dark, their thin cheeks mired
By their own blood—these Carriers and Héberts.
They only look so proud and so serene:
They only look so infinitely tired!

VICTOR PLARR.

BALLADE OF THE 'CHESHIRE CHEESE'
IN FLEET STREET

I KNOW a home of antique ease
    Within the smoky city's pale,
A spot wherein the spirit sees
    Old London through a thinner veil.
    The modern world, so stiff and stale,
You leave behind you, when you please,
    For long clay pipes and great old ale
And beefsteaks in the ' Cheshire Cheese.'

Beneath this board Burke's, Goldsmith's knees
    Were often thrust—so runs the tale—
'Twas here the Doctor took his ease,
    And wielded speech that, like a flail,
    Threshed out the golden truth : All hail
Great souls ! that met on nights like these,
    Till morning made the candles pale,
And revellers left the 'Cheshire Cheese.'

By kindly sense, and old decrees
    Of England's use, they set their sail—
We press to never-furrowed seas,
    For vision-worlds we breast the gale,

And still we seek and still we fail,
For still the 'glorious phantom' flees—-
   Ah, well ! no phantom are the ale
And beefsteaks of the 'Cheshire Cheese.'

Envoi

If doubts or debts thy soul assail,
   If Fashion's forms its current freeze,
Try a long pipe, a glass of ale,
   And supper in the 'Cheshire Cheese.'

                    T. W. ROLLESTON.

THE LAST MUSIC

CALMLY, breathe calmly all your music, maids!
Breathe a calm music over my dead queen.
All your lives long, you have nor heard, nor seen,
Fairer than she, whose hair in sombre braids
   With beauty overshades
   Her brow broad and serene.

Surely she hath lain so an hundred years:
Peace is upon her, old as the world's heart.
Breathe gently, music! Music done, depart:
And leave me in her presence to my tears,
   With music in mine ears;
   For sorrow hath its art.

Music, more music, sad and slow! She lies
Dead: and more beautiful than early morn.
Discrowned am I, and of her looks forlorn:
Alone vain memories immortalize
   The way of her soft eyes,
   Her virginal voice low-borne.

The balm of gracious death now laps her round,
As once life gave her grace beyond her peers.
Strange! that I loved this lady of the spheres,
To sleep by her at last in common ground:
       When kindly death hath bound
       Mine eyes, and sealed mine ears.

Maidens! make a low music: merely make
Silence a melody, no more. This day,
She travels down a pale and lonely way:
Now for a gentle comfort, let her take
       Such music, for her sake,
       As mourning love can play.

Holy my queen lies in the arms of death:
Music moves over her still face, and I
Lean breathing love over her. She will lie
In earth thus calmly, under the wind's breath:
       The twilight wind that saith:
       Rest! worthy found, to die.

                    LIONEL JOHNSON.

                    D

A DEATH IN THE FOREST

THE wind is loud among the trees to-night,
It sweeps the heavens where the stars are white.
I know : it is the angel with the sword.
Ah, not the woman, not the woman, Lord !

The wind is loud, I hear it in my brain,
I hear the rushing voices of the rain,
Hers in the rain, and his that once implored.
Ah, not the woman, not the woman, Lord !

Hands in the trees, hands in the flowing grass,
They wave to catch my spirit as I pass.
I have no hope to pass the ghastly ford.
Ah, not the woman, not the woman, Lord !

I see her tresses floating down the wind :
Her eyes are bright : it is for these I sinned.
We sinned, and I have had my own reward.
Ah, not the woman, not the woman, Lord !

She has a little mouth, a little chin :
God made her to be beautiful in sin,
God made her perfectly, to be adored.
Ah, not the woman, not the woman, Lord !

We sinned, but it is I who pay the price :
I say that she shall dwell in Paradise.
For me the feast in hell is on the board.
Ah, not the woman, not the woman, Lord !

ARTHUR SYMONS.

'ONLI DEATHE'

(Inscribed in an Old Ring)

'ONLY death us twain shall sever:'
'Nay, that he shall not do,' she saith:
'The Love I give you is for Ever:
 Dark Death for all his dire endeavour
 Decrees no parting—only death.'

ERNEST RADFORD.

AD DOMNULAM SUAM

LITTLE lady of my heart !
    Just a little longer,
Love me : we will pass and part,
    Ere this love grow stronger.

I have loved thee, Child ! too well,
    To do aught but leave thee :
Nay ! my lips should never tell
    Any tale, to grieve thee.

Little lady of my heart !
    Just a little longer,
I may love thee : we will part,
    Ere my love grow stronger.

Soon thou leavest fairy-land;
    Darker grow thy tresses :
Soon no more of hand in hand;
    Soon no more caresses !

Little lady of my heart !
    Just a little longer,
Be a child : then, we will part,
    Ere this love grow stronger.

                ERNEST DOWSON.

DEDICATION OF 'IRISH TALES'

THERE was a green branch hung with many a bell
  When her own people ruled in wave-worn Eri,
  And from its murmuring greenness, calm of faery
—A Druid kindness—on all hearers fell.

It charmed away the merchant from his guile,
  And turned the farmer's memory from his cattle,
  And hushed in sleep the roaring ranks of battle,
For all who heard it dreamed a little while.

Ah, Exiles wandering over many seas,
  Spinning at all times Eri's good to-morrow,
  Ah, world-wide Nation, always growing Sorrow,
I also bear a bell branch full of ease.

I tore it from green boughs winds tossed and hurled,
  Green boughs of tossing always, weary, weary,
  I tore it from the green boughs of old Eri,
The willow of the many-sorrowed world.

Ah, Exiles, wandering over many lands,
　My bell branch murmurs: the gay bells bring
　　laughter,
　Leaping to shake a cobweb from the rafter;
The sad bells bow the forehead on the hands.

A honied ringing, under the new skies
　They bring you memories of old village faces,
　Cabins gone now, old well-sides, old dear places,
And men who loved the cause that never dies.

                              W. B. YEATS.

QUATRAIN

THE EPITAPH ON HAFIZ, A YOUNG LINNET

DEAD here lies Hafiz, might have lived so long,
And turned his morning worm to morning song:
Now worms be glad, on Hafiz whet your teeth,
Until poor Hafiz' sexton lie beneath.

ERNEST RHYS.

JAVANESE DANCERS: A SILHOUETTE

TWITCHED strings, the clang of metal, beaten drums,
   Dull, shrill, continuous, disquieting;
And now the stealthy dancer comes
   Undulantly with cat-like steps that cling;

Smiling between her painted lids a smile
   Motionless, unintelligible, she twines
   Her fingers into mazy lines,
Twining her scarves across them all the while.

One, two, three, four, step forth, and, to and fro,
   Delicately and imperceptibly,
Now swaying gently in a row,
   Now interthreading slow and rhythmically,

Still with fixed eyes, monotonously still,
   Mysteriously, with smiles inanimate,
   With lingering feet that undulate,
With sinuous fingers, spectral hands that thrill,

The little amber-coloured dancers move,
   Like little painted figures on a screen,
   Or phantom dancers haply seen
Among the shadows of a magic grove.

                                        ARTHUR SYMONS.

CHORUS

(From Iphigeneia in Aulis) *

* Not a translation from Euripides.

Strophe

WHERE shall we find, in what remote
And dark abyss of time, the dread beginning
Of mortal woe: the crescent plague that smote
The germ of the world, the sin that set men sinning?
Or shall we blame for the evils of our state
Man's fatal fault, or faultful fate?
And why, and whence, and how begotten, came
That flying Mischief to the banquet-house,
Where the Olympians in divine carouse
Pledged Peleus and the silver-footed dame;
Till, shining there, the sudden fruit
Made spite in heaven: whence the contending Three
Naked in Ida; the bribed shepherd's flute
Cast by, and insolent rape launched on the sea,
And Helen and these wars; whence Peleus' son
Foredoomed, and no rest from calamity;
But woes in tireless tribe still raging on,
New sins, and innocent deaths?

Antistrophe

O, might we hear that song ye heard,
Ye pines, ye laurels, and thick-flowering myrtles,
On Pelion's flank, what time your leaves were stirr'd
With tuneful breath, when in their sacred kirtles
The Muses came over the mountain-side
To feast with Peleus and his bride !
For surely then they sang, the bright-haired Nine,
To the majestic tripping of their feet,
A nine-fold pæan, solemn, strange and sweet,
Of the ancient gods, and mysteries divine :
Fate and freewill, the hidden laws
That bind man's life; why good was doomed to be
Twin-born with evil; wherefore without pause
They strive; yet from their strife the harmony
That wakes new stars in heaven; yet, for our needs,
Heroes, and hearts that mould eternity,
And hopes that conquer fate, and noble deeds,
Virtues, and valorous deaths.

Epode

But, O ye Muses, who, since Time began
Most loved in heaven, most loving man,
Have talked with hoary Wisdom from your birth,
Sing to our inward ear, O sing again
That sage and solemn strain,

Make musical the riddle of the earth!
Make us to hear your ordered lyres
Ringing through chaos, wakening there
That world whereto, through vain desires
And woes, and strife, and much despair,
And many sins, the world aspires!

JOHN TODHUNTER.

TO A GREEK GEM

WAS it the signet of an Antonine—
This middle-finger ring, whose bezel glows
With the most lovely of intaglios
E'er wrought by craftsman in an age divine?
Or was it borne by grim Tiberius' line
At lustful festals and fierce wild beast shows?
Signed it wise edicts, or when Lucan chose
His artful liberal death was it the sign?

I cannot tell, nor can this lucent toy.
I only know that these small graven forms,
This cymbal-playing mænad and this boy,
In their delightful beauty shall live on,
Cranniéd 'mong crashing rocks, when Time's last
    storms
Have whelmed us in the sands we build upon.

VICTOR PLARR.

ARTS LOUGH

Glenmalure, Co. Wicklow

Lone lake half lost amidst encircling hills,
　　Beneath the imprisoning mountain-crags con-
　　　　cealed;
　　Who liest to the wide earth unrevealed;
To whose repose the brief and timorous rills

Bring scarce a murmur :—thou whose sight instils
　　Despair; o'er whom his dark disdainful shield
　　Abrupt Clogherna 'gainst the sun doth wield,
And thy dim face with deepening shadow fills :

O poet soul ! companionless and sad,
　　Tho' half the daytime long a death-like shade
　　Athwart thy depths with constant horror lies,

Thou art not ever in dejection clad,
　　But showest still, as in a glass displayed,
　　The limitless unfathomable skies.

　　　　　　　　　　G. A. Greene.

IN FALMOUTH HARBOUR

THE large, calm harbour lies below
Long, terraced lines of circling light :
Without, the deep sea currents flow :
   And here are stars, and night.

No sight, no sound, no living stir,
But such as perfect the still bay :
So hushed it is, the voyager
   Shrinks at the thought of day.

We glide by many a lanterned mast ;
Our mournful horns blow wild to warn
Yon looming pier : the sailors cast
   Their ropes, and watch for morn.

Strange murmurs from the sleeping town,
And sudden creak of lonely oars
Crossing the water, travel down
   The roadstead, the dim shores.

A charm is on the silent bay;
Charms of the sea, charms of the land.
Memories of open wind convey
    Peace to this harbour strand.

Far off, Saint David's crags descend
On seas of desolate storm: and far
From this pure rest, the Land's drear End,
    And ruining waters, are.

Well was it worth to have each hour
Of high and perilous blowing wind:
For here, for now, deep peace hath power
    To conquer the worn mind.

I have passed over the rough sea,
As over the white harbour bar:
And this Death's dreamland is to me,
    Led hither by a star.

And what shall dawn be? Hush thee, nay!
Soft, soft is night, and calm, and still:
Save that day cometh, what of day
    Knowest thou: good, or ill?

Content thee! Not the annulling light
Of any pitiless dawn is here;
Thou art alone with ancient night:
    And all the stars are clear.

Only the night air, and the dream;
Only the far, sweet smelling wave;
The stilly sounds, the circling gleam,
  Are thine : and thine the grave.

               LIONEL JOHNSON.

E

A CHOICE OF LIKENESSES

'Nay,' said the husband, 'give him this,'
   In manifest alarm,
'This is her very likeness;—that
   Has but a sudden charm.'

'The look that flashes into light
   And quickly dies away
   May blind some passer : as for me,
   I love the looks that stay.'

And I but said : (what could I say—
   Not dreaming any harm ?)
'They're yours, old friend, her looks that stay.
   Spare then to me—she surely may—
   This glance of sudden charm.'

                              Ernest Radford.

TO AUTUMN

THE year grows still again, the surging wake
  Of full-sailed summer folds its furrows up,
    As after passing of an argosy
    Old silence settles back upon the sea,
  And ocean grows as placid as a cup.
    Spring the young morn, and Summer the strong
        noon,
Have dreamed and done and died for Autumn's sake;
  Autumn that finds not for a loss so dear
    Solace in stack and garner hers too soon—
  Autumn, the faithful widow of the year.

Autumn, a poet once so full of song,
  Wise in all rhymes of blossom and of bud,
Hath lost the early magic of his tongue,
  And hath no passion in his failing blood.
Hear ye no sound of sobbing in the air?
  'Tis his,—low bending in a secret lane,
Late blooms of second childhood in his hair,

He tries old magic like a dotard mage;
  Tries spell and spell to weep and try again :
Yet not a daisy hears, and everywhere
      The hedgerow rattles like an empty cage.

He hath no pleasure in his silken skies,
  Nor delicate ardours of the yellow land;
Yea ! dead, for all its gold, the woodland lies,
  And all the throats of music filled with sand.
Neither to him across the stubble field
  May stack or garner any comfort bring,
    Who loveth more this jasmine he hath made,
  The little tender rhyme he yet can sing,
Than yesterday with all its pompous yield
  Or all its shaken laurels on his head.

                              RICHARD LE GALLIENNE.

VANITAS

BEYOND the need of weeping,
  Beyond the reach of hands,
May she be quietly sleeping,
  In what dim nebulous lands?
Ah, she who understands!

The long, long winter weather,
  These many years and days,
Since she, and Death, together,
  Left me the wearier ways:
.And now, these tardy bays!

The crown and victor's token:
  How are they worth to-day?
The one word left unspoken,
  It were late now to say:
But cast the palm away!

For once, ah once, to meet her,
  Drop laurel from tired hands;

Her cypress were the sweeter,
  In her oblivious lands :
Haply she understands!

Yet, crossed that weary river,
  In some ulterior land,
Or anywhere, or ever,
Will she stretch out a hand ?
  And will she understand ?

ERNEST DOWSON.

A FAIRY SONG

Sung by 'the Good People' over the outlaw Michael Dwyer and his bride, who had escaped into the mountains

WE who are old, old and gay,
  O so old,
Thousands of years, thousands of years,
  If all were told:

Give to these children new from the world
  Silence and love,
And the long dew-dropping hours of the night
  And the stars above:

Give to these children new from the world
  Rest far from men.
Is anything better, anything better?
  Tell it us then:

Us who are old, old and gay,
  O so old,
Thousands of years, thousands of years,
  If all were told.

W. B. YEATS.

MOTHERS OF MEN

WHEN fire and life are apart and twain,
And anger sleeps, and her sister pain,
And softly doses,—
His eyelid closes,—
The tired young love, and his wing reposes.

Then gather, like shades of the Earth's first mood
In a sweet and compassionate multitude,
Oh you who are old,
And whose eyes have told
The young wide eyes that their first light hold,—

Have loved, and have told of the long life-change,—
Why night is faithful, and daylight strange,—
How the dark increase
Of the seed called peace
Is the flower of hope, and the fruit release.

Come one, who art near me, and all set free,
Come forth from the earth, or the dull gray sea,
Come now, for a grace
In your light finds place
That weight cannot cover, nor dreams efface.

Come near, I would bend to you, mother of men,
Whose calm soft answering face again
Gives fear and joy
As when loves employ
The lips of the girl and the young-lipped boy.

Come near, for all mothers are near in you.
Make holy the lips and the eyes renew
That in youth have wandered
And favour squandered
In kisses unweighed and in tears unpondered.

Oh not by the morning, so sweet as now
In the maid-like droop of a bird-filled bough,
From the bough wind-stirred
Is a music heard,
Nor more shall the tree love the small brown bird.

Nor blue of the noon as revered, nor red
So loved in the wine of the sun, wide-spread,
Nor a child that laughed,
Nor a lightning shaft
More white, nor freer the white-sailed craft.

For you, oh mothers of men, are more
When the kiss bids open, and hearts outpour,
Than all of these,
Nor on lands nor seas
Shall love without your love bring me ease.

EDWIN J. ELLIS.

CHATTERTON IN HOLBORN

FROM country fields I came, that hid
    The harvest mice at play,
And followed care, whose calling bid
    To London's troubled way.

And there I wandered, far and wide,
    And came, ere day was done,
Where Holborn poured its civic tide
    Beneath the autumn sun.

So hot the sun, so great the throng,
    I gladly stayed my feet
To hear a captive linnet's song
    Accuse the London street.

Above, an ancient roof-tree bowed
    Its gabled head, and made
Obeisance to the modern crowd
    That swept athwart its shade.

Below, an open window kept
   Old books in grave array,
Where critics drowsed, and poets slept,
   Till Grub Street's judgment day.

One book I drew forth carelessly—
   The book of Rowley's rhyme,
That Chatterton, in seigneury
   Of song, bore out of time.

The merchant of such ware unseen,
   Watched spider-like the street,
He came forth, gray and spider-thin,
   And talked with grave conceit.

Old books, old times—he drew them nigh,
   At Chatterton's pale spell:
''Twas Brook Street yonder saw him die,
   Old Holborn knew him well.'

The words brought back in sudden sway
   That tale of poet's doom,
It seemed the boy but yesterday
   Died in his lonely room.

Without the press of men was heard,
   I heard, as one who dreamed,
The hurrying throng, the singing bird,
   And yesterday it seemed.

And as I turned to go, the tale
　　This pensive requiem made,
As though within the graveyard rail,
　　The boy was newly laid.

Requiem

Perhaps, who knows, the hurrying throng
　　Had hopeless signs for him;
I fancy how he wandered long
　　Until the light grew dim.

The windows saw him come and pass,
　　And come and go again;
And still the throng swept by—alas!
　　The barren face of men.

And when the day was gone, the way
　　Led down to the lethal deeps :
Sweet Life, what requiem to say?
　　'Tis well, 'tis well, he sleeps.

ERNEST RHYS.

TO A PASSIONIST

CLAD in a vestment wrought with passion flowers;
Celebrant of one Passion; called by name
Passionist : is thy world, one world with ours?
Thine, a like heart ?   Thy very soul, the same?

Thou pleadest an eternal sorrow: we
Praise the still changing beauty of this earth.
Passionate good and evil, thou dost see :
Our eyes behold the dreams of death and birth.

We love the joys of men: we love the dawn,
Red with the sun, and with the pure dew pearled.
Thy stern soul feels, after the sun withdrawn,
How much pain goes to perfecting the world.

Canst thou be right ?   Is thine the very truth ?
Stands then our life in so forlorn a state ?
Nay, but thou wrongest us; thou wrong'st our youth;
Who dost our happiness compassionate.

And yet ! and yet ! O royal Calvary !
Whence divine sorrow triumphed through years past !
Could ages bow before mere memory ?
Those passion flowers must blossom, to the last.

Purple they bloom, the splendour of a King :
Crimson they bleed, the sacrament of Death :
About our thrones and pleasaunces they cling,
Where guilty eyes read, what each blossom saith.

                                        LIONEL JOHNSON.

FREEDOM IN A SUBURB

He leaned upon the narrow wall
That set the limit to his ground,
And marvelled, thinking of it all,
That he such happiness had found.

There long he sat in perfect peace :
He smoked his pipe, he thanked his stars;
(His stars—unnumbered in the Lease);
He blest the subterranean cars

That bore him back the home to win
Where in the morn he'd left a heart
Not trusted in the devil's din
Of London's damnèd money mart.

ERNEST RADFORD.

QUATRAIN

LES BOURGEOISES

THEIR health they to their horses give :
  They, dully blinking, ride behind,
And yawn again, who do not live,
  But seek for life and never find.

ERNEST RHYS.

F

DRIFTING

As one that drifting in an open boat
  Down a broad river, singing, wayfareth,
While on the banks few listeners hear the note,

And pause and hearken, till the lapsing stream
  Seaward bears on the bark whence murmureth
Music that fails and dies, a flying dream:

Such is my song. Borne downward on the tide,
  I cannot tell what echoes of my breath
Are caught by listeners on the riverside:
  I and my songs glide onward unto death.

G. A. GREENE.

VILLANELLE OF SUNSET

COME hither, child ! and rest :
    This is the end of day,
Behold the weary West !
Sleep rounds with equal zest
    Man's toil and children's play :
Come hither, child ! and rest.
My white bird, seek thy nest,
    Thy drooping head down lay :
Behold the weary West !
Now are the flowers confest
    Of slumber: sleep, as they !
Come hither, child ! and rest.
Now eve is manifest,
    And homeward lies our way :
Behold the weary West !
Tired flower ! upon my breast,
    I would wear thee, alway :
Come hither, child ! and rest ;
Behold, the weary West !

               ERNEST DOWSON.

THE LAKE ISLE OF INNISFREE

I WILL arise and go now, and go to Innisfree,
    And a small cabin build there, of clay and wattles
       made;
Nine bean rows will I have there, a hive for the
      honey bee,
    And live alone in the bee-loud glade.

And I shall have some peace there, for peace comes
       dropping slow,
    Dropping from the veils of the morning to where
      the cricket sings;
There midnight's all a glimmer, and noon a purple
       glow,
    And evening full of the linnet's wings.

I will arise and go now, for always night and day
    I hear lake water lapping with low sounds on the
      shore;
While I stand on the roadway or on the pavements
      gray,
    I hear it in the deep heart's core.

W. B. YEATS.

A SUNDIAL—FLOWERS OF TIME

(In memory of R. A. L., Sculptor)

MARK how with loving hand he wrought
Here on the dial that counts the hours
Thy sad great figure ; wingèd Time
Set heavy-hearted mid the flowers.

Ah, even whilst he wrought did he
Close a great bargain with the years,
The sooner with these flowers to be
That for their nurture have thy tears.

ERNEST RADFORD.

TWILIGHT-PIECE

THE golden river-reach afar
  Kisses the golden skies of even,
And there's the first faint lover's star
  Alight along the walls of heaven.

The river murmurs to the boughs,
  The boughs make music each to each,
And still an amorous west wind soughs
  And loiters down the lonesome reach.

And here on the slim arch that spans
  The rippling stream, in dark outline,
You see the poor old fisherman's
  Bowed form and patient rod and line.

A picture better than all art,
  Since none could catch that sunset stain,
Or set in the soft twilight's heart
  This small strange touch of human pain !

VICTOR PLARR.

SUNSET IN THE CITY

Above the town a monstrous wheel is turning,
  With glowing spokes of red,
Low in the west its fiery axle burning;
  And, lost amid the spaces overhead,
A vague white moth, the moon, is fluttering.

Above the town an azure sea is flowing
  'Mid long peninsulas of shining sand,
From opal unto pearl the moon is growing,
  Dropped like a shell upon the changing strand.

Within the town the streets grow strange and
      haunted,
  And, dark against the western lakes of green,
The buildings change to temples, and unwonted
  Shadows and sounds creep in where day has been.

Within the town the lamps of sin are flaring,
  Poor foolish men that know not what ye are!
Tired traffic still upon his feet is faring—
  Two lovers meet and kiss, and watch a star.

                    RICHARD LE GALLIENNE.

AN EPITAPH

I DREAMED that one had died in a strange place
　　Near no accustomed hand,
And they had nailed the boards above her face,
　　The peasants of that land,
And wondering, planted by her solitude
　　A cypress and a yew.
I came and wrote upon a cross of wood
　　—Man had no more to do—
' She was more beautiful than thy first love
　　This lady by the trees,'
And gazed upon the mournful stars above
　　And heard the mournful breeze.

W. B. YEATS.

PROVERBS

COMFORT for the falling powers;
  Sorrow for the prime:
Breathing will for youthful hours;
  Later, written rhyme;—

Youth, a furious pondering,
  Hardly pardoning breath:
Age a sleep, with wandering;
  Dreams, the door of death.

Youth a wakening: life a cry:
  Age a sleep:—oh, age a sleep!
Silent loves eternally
  His midnight watches keep.

Silent loves and silent stars,
  'And he their silent guest,
While youth and rhyme, and pain and prime
  Serve his eternal rest.

EDWIN. J. ELLIS.

PLATO IN LONDON

THE pure flame of one taper fall
Over the old and comely page :
No harsher light disturb at all
This converse with a treasured sage.
Seemly, and fair, and of the best,
  If Plato be our guest,
  Should things befall.

Without, a world of noise and cold :
Here, the soft burning of the fire.
And Plato walks, where heavens unfold,
About the home of his desire.
From his own city of high things,
  He shows to us, and brings,
  Truth of fine gold.

The hours pass ; and the fire burns low ;
The clear flame dwindles into death:
Shut then the book with care ; and so,

Take leave of Plato, with hushed breath,
A little, by the falling gleams,
    Tarry the gracious dreams :
    And they too go.

Lean from the window to the air :
Hear London's voice upon the night !
Thou hast held converse with things rare :
Look now upon another sight !
The calm stars, in their living skies :
    And then, those surging cries,
    This restless glare !

That starry music, starry fire,
High above all our noise and glare :
The image of our long desire,
The beauty, and the strength, are there.
And Plato's thought lives, true and clear,
    In as august a sphere :
    Perchance, far higher.

LIONEL JOHNSON.

SONG OF THE SONGSMITHS

(*First Anniversary of the Rhymers' Club*)

Here do we meet again,
   After a full year's time:
Here do we meet again,
Meet with our old refrain,
   Praise of the regal rhyme.
Songsmiths like them who of old
Fashioned their speech of gold
   In a far, forgotten clime,
We at that ancient fire
With our young bright breath suspire,
   And hammer the golden rhyme,
   Hammer the ringing rhyme
     Till the echoes tire.

Who is it jeers at our song?
   Scoffs at an art sublime?
Who is it jeers at our song?
We who know right from wrong
   Worship the godlike rhyme.

Still on the world-wide breeze,
Over the surge of the seas,
   Comes like an echoed chime
The voice of all passions that play
In the dim heart of man alway,
   With the rush of a rolling rhyme,
   The lilt of a lulling rhyme,
      To the end of day.

Ours is the prentice-hand;
   Yet 'tis in us no crime,
Here in the misty land,
To seek for the fire that was fanned
   By kings of the kingly rhyme.
They have gone down to the shade,
Leaving the songs they made
   A wreath for the brows of Time.
Still is the great world young;
Not yet is the lyre unstrung,
   As it shakes to the quivering rhyme,
   Sighs for the resonant rhyme
      Of the songs unsung.

Ours are the echoes at least
   That fell from that golden prime;
Ours are the echoes at least,
Ours are the crumbs from the feast
   At the feet of the queenly rhyme :

Ours be the task to prolong
The joy and the sorrow of song
  In the mist of years that begrime;
In the clinging mist of the years,
With reverent toil and with tears,
  To hammer the golden rhyme,
  Hammer the ringing rhyme
    Till the mad world hears.

G. A. GREENE.

THE SECOND BOOK

OF

THE RHYMERS' CLUB

THE SECOND BOOK

OF

THE RHYMERS' CLUB

London: ELKIN MATHEWS & JOHN LANE
New York: DODD, MEAD & COMPANY
1894

THE RHYMERS' CLUB

ERNEST DOWSON

EDWIN J. ELLIS

G. A. GREENE

ARTHUR CECIL HILLIER

LIONEL JOHNSON

RICHARD LE GALLIENNE

VICTOR PLARR

ERNEST RADFORD

ERNEST RHYS

T. W. ROLLESTON

ARTHUR SYMONS

JOHN TODHUNTER

W. B. YEATS

Some of the following Poems have been published in various periodicals, *The Academy*, *The National Observer*, *The Spectator*, *The Bookman*, *Macmillan*, *The Hobby-Horse*, etc.; others again in *A Fellowship in Song*, in *Book-Song*, and in *A Light Load*. We are indebted to the various Editors for courteous permission to republish.

CONTENTS

PAGE

In Westminster Abbey : October 12,
    1892 .   .   .   .   .   *John Todhunter* .   .   1

Beyond ? .   .   .   .   .   *G. A. Greene*   .   .   3

Ad Cinerarium   .   .   .   *Victor Plarr*   .   .   4

Extreme Unction   .   .   .   *Ernest Dowson*   .   .   6

Solace (In Memoriam W. H. W.)   .   *Ernest Radford* .   .   8

Lost   .   .   .   .   .   *Ernest Radford* .   .   8

Mystic and Cavalier   .   .   *Lionel Johnson*   .   .   9

The Rose in My Heart   .   .   *W. B. Yeats*   .   .   11

Howel the Tall   .   .   .   *Ernest Rhys*   .   .   12

A Ballad of London .   .   .   *Richard Le Gallienne* .   20

Venus   .   .   .   .   *Edwin J. Ellis*   .   .   22

Nora on the Pavement   .   .   *Arthur Symons* .   .   23

Morning : Cycling Song .   .   *T. W. Rolleston* .   .   25

The Invasion of Brittany .   .   *Arthur Cecil Hillier* .   28

To a Breton Beggar .   .   .   *Victor Plarr*   .   .   30

Glories   .   .   .   .   *Lionel Johnson*   .   .   33

The Song of Tristram   .   .   *John Todhunter* .   .   34

			PAGE
To One in Bedlam	*Ernest Dowson*	.	3
Proserpine (For a Picture) .	*G. A. Greene*	.	3
The Folk of the Air . . .	*W. B. Yeats*	.	3
Song	*Ernest Radford*	.	40
Love's Exchange . . .	*Richard Le Gallienne*	.	4
In Excelsis	*Arthur Cecil Hillier*	.	43
Love and Art	*Arthur Symons*	.	45
A Year of the River . . .	*Edwin J. Ellis*	.	47
Noon-day (Elegiacs) . .	*T. W. Rolleston*	.	5
Song of the Wulfshaw Larches	*Ernest Rhys*	.	53
To Morfydd	*Lionel Johnson*	.	55
Deer in Greenwich Park . .	*Victor Plarr*	.	57
Non sum qualis eram bonae sub regno			
Cynarae	*Ernest Dowson*	.	60
Euthanasia (*fin de siècle*) . .	*John Todhunter*	.	62
'Violets Full'	*G. A. Greene*	.	64
The Second Crucifixion . .	*Richard Le Gallienne*	.	66
The Fiddler of Dooney . .	*W. B. Yeats*	.	68
Orpheus in Covent Garden .	*Arthur Cecil Hillier*	.	70
Song in the Labour Movement	*Ernest Radford*	.	72
Evening (Evensong) . .	*T. W. Rolleston*	.	73
Peace	*Edwin J. Ellis*	.	75
Song	*Arthur Symons*	.	77
Death and the Player . .	*Victor Plarr*	.	78
In Opera-land	*Arthur Cecil Hillier*	.	80
Growth	*Ernest Dowson*	.	83
Quatrains	*John Todhunter*	.	84
The Dark Angel . . .	*Lionel Johnson*	.	87

PAGE

A Mood ('They have taken away my Lord, and I know not where they have laid Him.') . . *G. A. Greene* . . 90

A Mystical Prayer to The Masters of the Elements—Finvarra, Feacra, and Caolte . . . . *W. B. Yeats* . . 91

Hesperides . . . . *Richard Le Gallienne* . 93

Acknowledgment : to H. E. T. . *Ernest Radford* . . 95

Night : After All . . . *T. W. Rolleston* . . 96

Saint Anthony . . . . *Edwin J. Ellis* . . 98

To O. E. . . . . . *Ernest Rhys* . . 99

A Variation Upon Love . . . *Arthur Symons* . . 100

A Secret of the Sea . . . *Victor Plarr* . . 101

In an Old Library . . . *John Todhunter* . . 103

The Garden of Shadow . . *Ernest Dowson* . . 105

The Memorial Garden . . *Arthur Cecil Hillier* . 106

The Cap and Bells . . . *W. B. Yeats* . . 108

The Coming of War . . *Lionel Johnson* . . 110

Lady Macbeth (For a Picture by John S. Sargent, A.R.A.) . . . *G. A. Greene* . . 113

Time's Monotone . . . *Richard Le Gallienne* . 114

The Shelley Memorial: The Master's Speech . . . . *Ernest Radford* . . 116

The Wail of the Decadent . . *Ernest Radford* . . 116

The Old Shepherd . . . *Edwin J. Ellis* . . 117

Midsummer Day . . . *Arthur Cecil Hillier* . 119

'Ah, dans ces mornes séjours Les jamais sont les toujours ' . . *Ernest Dowson* . . 120

					PAGE
On Great Sugarloaf	.	.	.	*G. A. Greene* .	. 122
Celtic Speech .	.	.	.	*Lionel Johnson* .	. 123
The Night-Jar	.	.	.	*Victor Plarr* .	. 124
The Song of the Old Mother .		.	.	*W. B. Yeats* .	. 126
The First Spring Day	.	.	.	*John Todhunter* .	. 127
An Ode to Spring .	.	.	.	*Richard Le Gallienne* .	129
A Presiding Examiner	.	.	.	*Ernest Radford* .	. 133
A Rhyme on Rhyme	.	.	.	*Edwin J. Ellis* .	. 135

THE RHYMERS' CLUB

IN WESTMINSTER ABBEY

October 12, 1892

In her still House of Fame her Laureate dead
  England entombs to-day, lays him to rest,
The leaves of honour green around his head,
    Love's flowers fresh on his breast.

Mourn him in solemn service of high song,
  Music serene as breathed in his last breath,
When, to the soundless ocean borne along,
    He met majestic Death.

Mourn him with grief's most fair solemnities,
  Ritual that with an inward rapture suits,
While in stern pomp the mind's grave companies
    March, as to Dorian flutes.

A

If tears we shed, 'tis but as eyes grow dim
   When some rich strain superbly rolls away,
For like the close of an Olympian hymn
      Ended his golden day.

Bear him in pride, like a dead conqueror
   Brought home to his last triumph in sad state,
Over him his Country's Flag, who in life's war
      Was victor over fate.

We saw him stand, a lordly forest tree,
   His branches filled with music, all the air
Glad for his presence; fallen at last is he,
      And all the land is bare.

So, with old Handel thundering in our ears,
   His mighty dirge marching from breast to breast
In sorrow's purple pageant, with proud tears
      We leave him to his rest.

                  JOHN TODHUNTER.

BEYOND?

WHAT lies beyond the splendour of the sun,
   Beyond his flashing belt of sister-spheres?
   What deeps are they whereinto disappears
The visitant comet's sword, of fire fine-spun?

What rests beyond the myriad lights that run
   Their nightly race around our human fears?
   Hope-signals raised on multitudinous spears
Of armies captained by the Eternal One?

Beyond the sun, and far beyond the stars,
   Beyond the weariness of this our day,
Beyond this fretting at the prison-bars,
   The urgent soul, divine in soulless clay,
Bids us set forth, through endless avatars,
   To seek where God hath hidden Himself away.

G. A. GREENE.

AD CINERARIUM

Who in this small urn reposes,
Celt or Roman, man or woman,
Steel of steel, or rose of roses?

Whose the dust set rustling slightly,
In its hiding-place abiding,
When this urn is lifted lightly?

Sure some mourner deemed immortal
What thou holdest and enfoldest,
Little house without a portal!

When the artificers had slowly
Formed thee, turned thee, sealed thee, burned thee,
Freighted with thy burden holy,

Sure, he thought, 'there's no forgetting
All the sweetness and completeness
Of such rising, of such setting,'

And so bade them grave no token,
Generation, age, or nation,
On thy round side still unbroken,—

Let them score no cypress verses,
Funeral glories, prayers, or stories,
Mourner's tears, or mourner's curses,

Round thy brown rim time hath polished;—
Left thee dumbly cold and comely
As some shrine of gods abolished.

Ah 'twas well!   It scarcely matters
What is sleeping in the keeping
Of this house of mortal tatters,—

Steel of steel, or rose of roses,
Man or woman, Celt or Roman,
If but soundly he reposes !

                              VICTOR PLARR.

EXTREME UNCTION

Upon the lips, the eyes, the feet,
   On all the passages of sense,
The atoning oil is spread with sweet
   Renewal of lost innocence.

The feet that lately ran so fast
   To meet desire, are soothly sealed:
The eyes, that were so often cast
   On vanity, are touched and healed.

From troublous sights and sounds set free,
   In such a twilight hour of breath,
Shall one retrace his life, or see
   Through shadows the true face of Death?

Vials of mercy! sacring oils!
   I know not where, nor when I come,
Nor through what wanderings and toils
   To crave of you Viaticum.

Yet when the walls of flesh grow weak,
   In such an hour, it well may be,
Through mist and darkness light shall break,
   And each anointed sense shall see !

ERNEST DOWSON.

SOLACE
(*In Memoriam W. H. W.*)

HE worketh still.
Superior to Death's smart
   He worketh still.
What his spent years could not fulfil
I shall endeavour for my part:
For ever, living in my heart,
   He worketh still.

ERNEST RADFORD.

LOST

SOMETHING has gone.
Oh life, great giver as thou art,
   Something has gone.
Not love, for love as years roll on
Plays evermore a fuller part.
But of the treasure of my heart
   Something has gone.

ERNEST RADFORD.

MYSTIC AND CAVALIER

Go from me: I am one of those, who fall.
What! hath no cold wind swept your heart at all,
In my sad company?   Before the end,
        Go from me, dear my friend!

Yours are the victories of light: your feet
Rest from good toil, where rest is brave and sweet:
But after warfare in a mourning gloom,
        I rest in clouds of doom.

Have you not read so, looking in these eyes?
Is it the common light of the pure skies,
Lights up their shadowy depths?   The end is set:
        Though the end be not yet.

When gracious music stirs, and all is bright,
And beauty triumphs through a courtly night;
When I too joy, a man like other men:
        Yet, am I like them, then?

And in the battle, when the horsemen sweep
Against a thousand deaths, and fall on sleep:
Who ever sought that sudden calm, if I
     Sought not? yet could not die!

Seek with thine eyes to pierce this crystal sphere:
Canst read a fate there, prosperous and clear?
Only the mists, only the weeping clouds,
     Dimness and airy shrouds.

Beneath, what angels are at work? What powers
Prepare the secret of the fatal hours?
See! the mists tremble, and the clouds are stirred:
     When comes the calling word?

The clouds are breaking from the crystal ball,
Breaking and clearing: and I look to fall.
When the cold winds and airs of portent sweep,
     My spirit may have sleep.

O rich and sounding voices of the air!
Interpreters and prophets of despair:
Priests of a fearful sacrament! I come,
     To make with you mine home.

LIONEL JOHNSON.

THE ROSE IN MY HEART

ALL things uncomely and broken, all things worn out
    and old,
  The cry of a child by the roadway, the creak of
    a lumbering cart,
The heavy steps of the ploughman splashing the
    winter mould,
  Are wronging your image that blossoms a rose in
    the deeps of my heart.

The wrong of the things misshapen is wrong too great
    to be told;
  I hunger to build them anew, and sit on a green
    knoll apart,
With the earth, and the sky, and the water, re-made
    like a casket of gold
  For my dreams of your image that blossoms a rose
    in the deeps of my heart.

W. B. YEATS.

HOWEL THE TALL

I

Hawk of war, Howel the Tall,
      Prince of men :
Dead is Howel, David slew him;
He will not lead to war again !

Periv once, Kedivor's son,
      Sang him so,
Sang his youth and death and passion,
Now nine centuries ago.

But they say—the bardic poets,
      In their tales :
Whoso names in rhyme those heroes,
Calls them back again to Wales :

Calls them back, and gives them there
      Life and breath
In the grey and ancient places,
Where they gave their hearts to Death.

And this broken rhyme is made
  For a spell,
From the shades to summon Howel
To the land he loved so well.

II

Owain loved an Irish princess :
  So there sprang
Howel of two passionate races,
When harp and sword in Argoed rang.

Owain Gwyned, golden sire
  Of seven sons,
Fathered him: when Death took Owain,
Seven claimed the crown at once.

First-born of the seven, blighted
  Yorweth came;
Then David of the dagger-stroke,
And Madoc of the sailor's fame.

David's fingers felt the crown,
  And he said,
' Yorweth of the broken face;—
Ere he reign, be David dead ! '

Blighted Yorweth might not reign,
          Wanting grace:
Then the swords rang out for Howel,
For the beauty of his face.

Hawk of war! Howel ruled them
          Royally:
But his mother's blood was in him;
One morn he sailed the Irish Sea.

O, high the Gaelic welcome
          Of her house,
When he stayed to share the feasting
At their Lammas-tide carouse.

All too long indeed, while David,
          Left at home,
Plied Argoed with fine fury—
'Base-born Howel well may roam :

'Not for me this bastard bred
          Shall be King,
To come anon with Irishry
Of his mother's nurturing :

'Out my sword!' As swift the word,
        Winged with fate,
  Over sea was sped to Howel :—
  Come, or yet it be too late!

  Through the night the horsemen came,
        Spurring west :
'Hawk of war, arouse ! the ravens
  Pick to shreds your mountain nest !'

  Howel's horn broke up the feast :
        All the night
  They galloped thro' the Gadael's fields,
  And reached the sea at morning light.

  As he rode, at Howel's heart
        Stirred the strain,
  That he sang them while they waited
  For the ship to Porth Dinlleyn.

HOWEL'S SONG

  A foaming wave flows o'er the grave
        Where Rhivawn lies;
  Ah, I love the land beyond Arvon,
  Where the trefoil grows and the mountains rise.

I love at eve the seaward stream
Where the seamews brood,
And the famous vale of Cwm Dythore,
Where the nightingale sings in the privet wood

I love the land where we drank the mead,
And drove the spear,
At the forest side of Tegenyl,
Where my yellow steed outdid the deer;

Where Hunyd's love, and Gwen's white arm,
Defend my doom;
Where Olwen is, and Gwenerys,
And Nesta like the apple-bloom!

A foaming wave cried out all night
Upon my fate;
Last night I dreamt of an open grave,
A crying wound, and a closing gate.

A foaming wave flows o'er the grave
Of Rhivawn's sleep:
But dig my grave at the forest side,
Where the trefoils grow, and the squirrels leap!

III

There sang the heart whose even-song
      Came too true,
That soon lay rent on Arvon field
By David's dagger through and through.

Dead is the Prince of Chivalry;
      But Kymric rhyme
May call him yet to Argoed,
'Tis said, as of old time.

The shepherd there, at nightfall,
      O'er his sheep
Humming some old warlike rhyme,
May see him cross the steep.

There, late I climbed from Cwm Dythore
      The triple height,
To wait beside the mountain cairn
The ancient mystery of night.

The mountain drew his purple robe
      Around,
And his seven tireless torrents
Sent from the Cwm a lonely sound.

B

From the haunted vale of Howel
     At my feet,
I surely heard his even-song
Rise mountain-wild and sweet?—

'I love at eve the seaward stream,
     Where the seamews brood;
And the famous vale of Cwm Dythore,
Where the nightingale sings in the privet wood!'

And surely here, beside the cairn,
     A shadowy form
Gazes afar on Arvon field,
Where the cottage fires shine warm?

His mien heroic, round his brow
     The circling bay;
Around his neck the golden torque
Finds his dark locks half-way?

       *   *   *   *   *

So come the stars, so come and go,
     And he was gone;
Poised high, amid the mountain-night,
Beneath the stars, I stood alone.

But down the track the shepherds take,
    As I clung
On the torrent's brink, benighted,
And the mountain-fox gave tongue—

Night, nor Time, nor David's dagger,
    Could give pause
To your deathless rhyme, O Howel,
And, O Wales, your ancient cause !

ERNEST RHYS.

A BALLAD OF LONDON

Ah, London! London! our delight,
Great flower that opens but at night,
Great City of the midnight sun,
Whose day begins when day is done.

Lamp after lamp against the sky
Opens a sudden beaming eye,
Leaping alight on either hand,
The iron lilies of the Strand.

Like dragonflies, the hansoms hover,
With jewelled eyes, to catch the lover,
The streets are full of lights and loves,
Soft gowns, and flutter of soiled doves.

The human moths about the light
Dash and cling close in dazed delight,
And burn and laugh, the world and wife,
For this is London, this is life!

Upon thy petals butterflies,
But at thy root, some say, there lies,
A world of weeping trodden things,
Poor worms that have not eyes or wings.

From out corruption of their woe
Springs this bright flower that charms us so,
Men die and rot deep out of sight
To keep this jungle-flower bright.

Paris and London, World-Flowers twain
Wherewith the World-Tree blooms again,
Since Time hath gathered Babylon,
And withered Rome still withers on.

Sidon and Tyre were such as ye,
How bright they shone upon the tree!
But Time hath gathered, both are gone,
And no man sails to Babylon.

Ah, London! London! our delight,
For thee, too, the eternal night,
And Circe Paris hath no charm
To stay Time's unrelenting arm.

RICHARD LE GALLIENNE.

VENUS

UNSEEN forever, save by her own boy—
   And he is love, the ever blind and young,
   Blind by the light of his own youth out-flung—
Venus, the daughter of the whole world's joy,
Whom wisdom cannot hide nor years annoy,
   Like the bright sea whereout her birth is sprung,
   Still dances to her praise for ever sung,
And lives to laugh, to save and to destroy.
   But now, some say, she has returned again,
Being unseen, to her deep sleep in bliss.
   No, no ; while there are women loved of men,
As this is loved—and this is loved—and this—
   Venus returns no more beneath the sea :
   Seek her not there, for this—and this is she.

EDWIN J. ELLIS.

NORA ON THE PAVEMENT

As Nora on the pavement
Dances, and she entrances the grey hour
Into the laughing circle of her power,
The magic circle of her glances,
As Nora dances on the midnight pavement;

Petulant and bewildered,
Thronging desires and longing looks recur,
And memorably re-incarnate her,
As I remember that old longing,
A footlight fancy, petulant and bewildered;

There where the ballet circles,
See her, but ah, not free her from the race
Of glittering lines that link and interlace ;
This colour now, now that, may be her,
In the bright web of those harmonious circles.

But what are these dance measures,
Leaping and joyous, keeping time alone
With life's capricious rhythm, and all her own,
Life's rhythm and hers, long sleeping,
That wakes, and knows not why, in these danc
    measures ?

It is the very Nora;
Child, and most blithe, and wild as any elf,
And innocently spendthrift of herself,
And guileless and most unbeguiled,
Herself at last, leaps free the very Nora.

It is the soul of Nora,
Living at last, and giving forth to the night,
Bird-like, the burden of its own delight,
All its desire, and all the joy of living,
In that blithe madness of the soul of Nora.

                              ARTHUR SYMONS.

MORNING

CYCLING SONG

N the airy whirling wheel is the springing strength
        of steel
  And the sinew grows to steel day by day,
'ill you feel your pulses leap at the easy swing and
        sweep
  As the hedges flicker past upon the way.
        Then it's out to the kiss of the morning breeze,
            And the rose of the morning sky,
        And the long brown road where the tired spirit's
            load
          Slips off as the leagues go by.

lack and silver, swift and strong, with a pleasant
        undersong
  From the steady rippling murmur of the chain—

Half a thing of life and will, you may feel it start and
    thrill
  With a quick elastic answer to the strain
    As you ride to the kiss of the morning breeze,
      And the rose of the morning sky,
    And the long brown road where the tired spirit'
      load
      Slips off as the leagues go by.

Miles a hundred you may run from the rising of the
    sun
  To the gleam of the first white star;
You may ride through twenty towns, meet the sun
    upon the downs
  Or the wind on the mountain scaur.
    Then it's out to the kiss of the morning breeze
      And the rose of the morning sky,
    And the long brown road where the tired spirit'
      load
      Slips off as the leagues go by.

Down the pleasant country side, through the wood
    land's summer pride
  You have come in your forenoon spin—
And you never would have guessed how delicious is
    the rest
  In the shade by the wayside inn,

When you've sought the kiss of the morning
        breeze,
    And the rose of the morning sky,
And the long brown road where the tired spirit's
        load
    Slips off as the leagues go by.

Oh, there's many a one who teaches that the shining
        river reaches
  Are the place to spend a long June day.
But give me the whirling wheel and a boat of air and
        steel
  To float upon the Queen's highway !
        Oh give me the kiss of the morning breeze,
            And the rose of the morning sky,
        And the long brown road where the tired spirit's
                load
            Slips off as the leagues go by.

                            T. W. ROLLESTON.

THE INVASION OF BRITTANY

In fair Queen Paris, beneath the trees,
'Mid a blaze of cafés, a throng of men,
Whose speech tossed up on the warm night breeze
Is scattered like spray ere it rise again,
I have loitered forgotten and yet been fain
Of the Queen of the world and her sorceries,
But to-day she has filled up her cup in vain,
For our way to the Breton seaboard lies.

In old German woodlands, many a day,
I have lost myself to lie at peace,
'Mid the trooping pines, where the children play,
Till the light grows faint and the shadows increase,
And the cloud-drift hangs in a rose-bloom fleece
Where the dim blue Saxon highlands rise,
But, cease from thy spells, O Elbeland, cease,
For our way to the Breton seaboard lies.

In waking dreams I have travelled far
By swamps where the yellow reeds grow free,
Where India sits on a jewelled car
Or the spice-winds blow over Araby;
Chrysanthemum country were fair to see
And dainty its maids with the almond eyes,
But dreams must fade when the stars decree,
And our way to the Breton seaboard lies.

In the narrow streets of the grey old town
The gables tower to meet the skies,
And the windworn bastions grimly frown
On the strand where the Breton seaboard lies.

ARTHUR CECIL HILLIER.

TO A BRETON BEGGAR

(Dol Cathedral)

In the brown shadow of the transept door,
  Grey kings and granite prophets overhead,
Which are so ancient they can age no more,
  A beggar begs his bread.

He too is old,—so old, and worn, and still,
  He seems a part of those gaunt sculptures there,
By wizard masons dowered with power and will
  To moan sometimes in prayer :—

To moan in prayer, moving thin carven lips,
  And with faint senses striving to drink in
Some golden sound which peradventure slips
  From the altar's heart within.

What is thy prayer ?   Is it a plaintive praise,
  An intercession, or an anguished plaint;
Remorse, O sinner, for wild vanished days,
  Or ecstasy, O saint ?

And through long hours, when thou art wont to sit
    In moveless silence, what inspires thy thought?
Is thine an utter drowsing; or shall wit
    Still travail, memory-fraught?

Hear'st thou old battles?   Wast thou one of those
    Whose angry fire-locks made the hillsides ring,
When, clad in skins and rags, the Chouans rose
    To die for Church and King?

Or dost thou view, in weird and sad array,
    The long-dead Cymry—they of whom men tell
That always to the war they marched away,
    And that they always fell?

So moving are thine eyes which cannot see,
    So great a resignation haunts thy face,
I often think that I behold in thee
    The symbol of thy race:

Not as it was when bards Armorican
    Sang the high pageant of their Age of Gold;
But as it is, a sombre long-tressed man,
    Exceeding poor and old.

With somewhat in his eyes for some to read,
  Albeit dimmed with years and scarcely felt,—
The mystery of an antique deathless Creed,
  The glamour of the Celt.

VICTOR PLARR.

GLORIES

Roses from Paestan rosaries !
More goodly red and white was she :
Her red and white were harmonies,
Not matched upon a Paestan tree.

Ivories blaunched in Alban air !
She lies more purely blaunched than you :
No Alban whiteness doth she wear,
But death's perfection of that hue.

Nay ! now the rivalry is done,
Of red, and white, and whiter still :
She hath a glory from that sun,
Who falls not from Olympus hill.

LIONEL JOHNSON.

C

THE SONG OF TRISTRAM

THE star of love is trembling in the west,
 Night hears the desolate sea with moan on moan
 Sigh for the storm, who on his mountains lone
Smites his wild harp and dreams of her wild breast.
   I am thy storm, Isolt, and thou my sea !
    Isolt !
   My passionate sea!

The storm to her wild breast, the passionate sea
 To his fierce arms : we to the rapturous leap
 Of mated spirits mingling in love's deep,
Flame to flame, I to thee and thou to me !
   Thou to mine arms, Isolt, I to thy breast !
    Isolt !
   I to thy breast !

JOHN TODHUNTER.

TO ONE IN BEDLAM

WITH delicate, mad hands, behind his sordid bars,
Surely he hath his posies, which they tear and twine ;
Those scentless wisps of straw, that miserably line
His strait, caged universe, whereat the dull world stares,

Pedant and pitiful.   O, how his rapt gaze wars
With their stupidity!   Know they what dreams divine
Lift his long, laughing reveries like enchanted wine,
And make his melancholy germane to the stars' ?

O lamentable brother ! if those pity thee,
Am I not fain of all thy lone eyes promise me;
Half a fool's kingdom, far from men who sow and reap,
All their days, vanity ?   Better than mortal flowers,
Thy moon-kissed roses seem : better than love or sleep,
The star-crowned solitude of thine oblivious hours!

ERNEST DOWSON.

PROSERPINE

(For a Picture)

RULER of Darkness, Queen of desolate Night,
    Thee whom the innumerable Dead salute
    With myriad-murmuring homage, thee the fruit
Red-riven dooms to banishment from light.

Farewell, Sicilian orchards flowerful-bright !
    Farewell, the smiling of the sun ! no lute
    Of Orpheus shall revoke thee from the mute
Sad shadow-realm where thou art lapped in night.

Thee those far voices that thy name repeat,
    Charm not, with bent ear listening; nor thine eyes
    Wild like a fawn's, seek Enna's flowers and wheat

For thou hast found more fair the sunless skies,
    More blest the royalty of Death, more sweet
His love whose lone domain in darkness lies.

G. A. GREENE.

THE FOLK OF THE AIR

O'DRISCOLL drove with a song
  The wild duck and the drake
From the tall and the tufted reeds
  Of the drear Heart Lake.

,And he saw how the reeds grew dark
  At the coming of night tide,
And dreamed of the long dim hair
  Of Bridget his bride.

He heard while he sang and dreamed
  A piper piping away,
And never was piping so sad,
  And never was piping so gay.

And he saw young men and young girls
  Who danced on a level place,
And Bridget his bride among them,
  With a sad and a gay face.

The dancers crowded about him,
    And many a sweet thing said,
And a young man brought him red wine,
    And a young girl white bread.

But Bridget drew him by the sleeve,
    Away from the merry bands,
To old men playing at cards
    With a twinkling of ancient hands.

The bread and the wine had a doom,
    For these were the folk of the air;
He sat and played in a dream
    Of her long dim hair.

He played with the merry old men,
    And thought not of evil chance,
Until one bore Bridget his bride
    Away from the merry dance.

He bore her away in his arms,
    The handsomest young man there,
And his neck and his breast and his arms
    Were drowned in her long dim hair.

O'Driscoll got up from the grass
  And scattered the cards with a cry;
But the old men and dancers were gone
  As a cloud faded into the sky.

He knew now the folk of the air,
  And his heart was blackened by dread,
And he ran to the door of his house;
  Old women were keening the dead;

But he heard high up in the air
  A piper piping away;
And never was piping so sad,
  And never was piping so gay.

                              W. B. YEATS.

SONG

Oh what know they of harbours
Who toss not on the sea !
They tell of fairer havens,
But none so fair there be

As Plymouth town outstretching
Her quiet arms to me,
Her breast's broad welcome spreading
From Mewstone to Penlee.

Ah with this home-thought, darling,
Come crowding thoughts of thee—
Oh, what know they of harbours
Who toss not on the sea !

ERNEST RADFORD.

LOVE'S EXCHANGE

SIMPLE am I, I care no whit
　　For pelf or place,
It is enough for me to sit
　　And watch Dulcinea's face;
To mark the lights and shadows flit
Across the silver moon of it.

I have no other merchandise,
　　No stocks or shares,
No other gold but just what lies
　　In those deep eyes of hers ;
And, sure, if all the world were wise,
It too would bank within her eyes.

I buy up all her smiles all day,
　　With all my love,
And sell them back, cost price, or, say,
　　A kiss or two above;
It is a speculation fine,
The profit must be always mine.

The world has many things, 'tis true,
    To fill its time,
Far more important things to do
    Than making love and rhyme;
Yet, if it asked me to advise,
I'd say buy up Dulcinea's eyes !

RICHARD LE GALLIENNE.

IN EXCELSIS

Above the world at our window seat
All the murmur of London rises high,
From the hansoms racing along the street,
And the flaring stalls and the passers-by.

As the lamps of a rolling carriage gleam
You may catch for a moment a woman's face,
And a soft-robed figure—a vanishing dream
Of a white burnoose and a flutter of lace.

One argent star o'er the clock-tower wakes
More pure than the spark of a Northern night,
Where the sleeping woodlands and lonely lakes
Wed the splendour of frost to the glory of light.

Above the world at our window-sill
O'er the countless roofs of the city of care,
The darkness falls, and my pulses thrill
At the touch of thy cheek and the scent of thine hair.

We have lived here long through the dreary days
Of the sun and the rain and the trodden snow :
We have watched of an evening the heaven ablaze
With the smoky glare of the afterglow.

We have lived together and known great joys
And have sorrowed for much beyond recall,
And been soiled with the dust and deafened with noise,
And the crowd heeds not, but the stars know all.

ARTHUR CECIL HILLIER.

LOVE AND ART

THE sun went indistinguishably down
   Over the murky town,
Night droops about the houses heavily;
   The Temple gateways gape and frown,
But, as I enter, strangely, comes to me
The odour of patchouli.

Ah, there she flits before me, whose gay scent
   Betrays the way she went;
A corner intercepts her, she is gone;
   And as I follow, indolent,
My visiting mind, with her to muse upon,
Runs curiously on.

I seem to hear her mount the narrow stair,
   Creaking, for all her care,
And now a door flies open, just above,
   And now she laughs, to see him there,
His arms about her, and both babble of
The nonsense-verse of love.

I enter and forget them, for to-night
  I have my verse to write,
That love-song, I have yet to pare and trim.
  So, should it be ? or—God ! the light
In that revealing casement-square grows dim :
He kisses her, and I but write of him !

ARTHUR SYMONS.

A YEAR OF THE RIVER

THE Spring is here, the Spring is free
From bonds of Winter's jealousy,
The river is alive to-day :
She puts on blue, and puts off grey :
She laughs, and dances, and puts on
The daisies, and the dazzling swan,
The leaping moon along her waves,
And merrier foam that bounds and raves.

And now she rolls the buds, and now
The buds are leaves ; the willows bow.
The chestnuts fling their white ; the May
Comes hastening in the same glad day,
Till mightier strength of Summer's hand
Opens new heavens above our land,
And all the gifts the world has known
Return, like birds a moment flown.

I shared the day with every bird,
And what the kingfisher has heard
I heard, and saw in Summer noon
The little splash, the ripple's moon.
And evening with her golden space
That makes the swallow's darting place
Has widened out her peace for me
And watched her children silently.

Then call me not away while yet
No frost, nor storms, nor mists have met
Nor sorrow paints the world in grey,
Nor labour lives at war with day,
Or night is dark as sepulture,
While rattling trees affright the shore
With semblances of deathly bones,
And wind bewails in undertones.

For, even then, in lighted rooms
I feel at heart the unheeded glooms
Where—through a humble moon and pale
Wanders along the windy vale
And labours with the heavy stress
Of cloudy motion limitless,
Like sorrow where I feel no part,
And yet that whispers near my heart.

Oh come but once, come out alone
And see what secret thing is known
In silence of the winter stream.
She needs no pity in her dream;
She only wears the face of grief
As Summer with the golden sheaf
Puts on the mask of joy awhile
And bids our easy hours to smile.

But here the shadow owns an art
That teaches each o'er-tired heart
A skill unknown to noisy Spring,
Unknown to Summer on the wing,
Unknown to Autumn satisfied,
The art to see, and stand aside;
To look on grief as only grief,
And death as but a fallen leaf.

Here Spring, impatient of her tears,
Here Summer, wrath in weeping years
And flinging thunder upon rain,
Here Autumn numbering her grain,
And busy in her golden stores,
While hour by hour the sorrow pours
That grieves the fading of the year,
All these are dumb and foolish here.

D

But wintry night and solitude
That lean upon the stream to brood
Hold silence deep to float the word
Across the inspired spaces heard
Between the stars, beyond the gloom
Of years that in the eternal womb
Are not as yet brought forth for tears:
Then we make peace with our brief years.

I hear her as the midnight weeps,
I hear her as the echo sleeps
Forgetting what the Spring bird knows,
I hear her as the quiet flows;
And who shall come with me to roam
Along her shore, shall turn to home
And bring a quiet thing like this,
The patient River will not miss.

EDWIN J. ELLIS.

NOON-DAY

Elegiacs

WIND, O wind of the Spring, thine old enchantment
    renewing,
  How at the shock of thy might wakens a cry within
    me!
Out of what wonderful lands never trodden by man,
    never told of,
  Lands where never a ship anchored or trafficker
    fared,
Comest thou, breathing like flame till the brown earth
    flames into blossom,
  Quickening the sap of old woods swayed in thy stormy
    embrace,
Rousing in depths of the heart the wild waves of an
    infinite longing,
  Longing for freedom and life, longing for Springs that
    are dead?

Surely the far blue sea, foam-flecked with the speed of
    thy coming,
  Brightened in laughter abroad, sang at the feet of
    the isles,
Stirred in a tumult of joy, as my soul stirs trembling
    with passion,
  Trembling with passion and hope, wild with the
    spirit of Spring.
Ah, what dreams rearise, half pain half bliss to re-
    member,
  Hearing the storm of thy song, blown from the
    height of the skies :
Something remains upon earth to be done, to be dared,
    to be sought for.
  Up with the anchor again! out with the sails to the
    blast!
Out to the shock of the seas that encircle the Fortunate
    Islands,
  Vision and promise and prize, home of the Wind of
    the Spring!

T. W. ROLLESTON.

SONG OF THE WULFSHAW LARCHES

HEART of Earth, let us be gone,
From this rock where we have stayed
While the sun has risen and shone
Ten thousand times, and thrown our shade
Always in the self-same place.

Now the night draws on apace :
The day is dying on the height,
The wind brings cold sea-fragrance here,
And cries, and restless murmurings,
Now night is near,—
Of wings and feet that take to flight,
Of furry feet and feathery wings
That take their joyous flight at will
Away and over the hiding hill,
And into the land where the sun has fled.

O let us go, as they have sped,—
The soft swift shapes that left us here,
The gentle things that came and went
And left us in imprisonment !
Let us be gone, as they have gone,
Away, and into the hidden lands;—
From rock and turf our roots uptear,
Break from the clinging keeping bands,
Out of this long imprisoning break;
At last, our sunward journey take,
And far, to-night, and farther on,—
Heart of Earth, let us be gone !

ERNEST RHYS.

TO MORFYDD

A VOICE on the winds,
A voice by the waters,
  Wanders and cries :

Oh! what are the winds?
And what are the waters?
  Mine are your eyes.

Western the winds are,
And western the waters,
  Where the light lies :

Oh! what are the winds?
And what are the waters?
  Mine are your eyes!

Cold, cold, grow the winds,
And dark grow the waters,
  Where the sun dies :

Oh! what are the winds?
And what are the waters?
  Mine are your eyes!

And down the night winds,
And down the night waters,
  The music flies:

Oh! what are the winds?
And what are the waters?
Cold be the winds,
And wild be the waters,
  So mine be your eyes!

LIONEL JOHNSON.

DEER IN GREENWICH PARK

PATHETIC in their rags, from far and near,
    The children of the slum o'er-swarm the grass :
Pathetic in their grace, the Greenwich deer
    Leap up to let them pass.

Where riot scares the gloom, and fevers burn,
    These wizened babes were pent till morning light :
Slim shadows moving 'mong the moonlit fern
    The shy deer strayed all night.

In the hot hours London's poor wastrels find
    Their paradise in this brown London park :
The lordlier brutes, in the scant shade reclin'd,
    Pant for the hours of dark,

When some dim instinct from primæval years
    Thrills, on a sudden, through each dappled breast,
And with untameable mysterious fears
    The herd is re-possessed !

Then the branch'd horns are tossed; the nostrils fine
   Respire the sleepy breath from London's heart,
And bucks, and does, and fawns, in spectral line,
   Forth from their bracken start.

An antlered watchman stamps a shapely hoof :
   —Is that a tartan'd Gael within the brake ?
Did Luath bay below the heath-clad roof—
   Doth Fingal's son awake ?

Hath a harp wailed in Tara ?   Did a bough
   Snap in Broceliande, where Merlin keeps
His drowsy magic vigil even now
   In the oakwood's sunlit deeps ?

Was it a cry borne from Caerluda town,—
   A spell the Stag of Ages understands ?
Or voices of old rivers raving down
   Through many heathery lands ?

Or—since the red stag by wild mountain streams
   Is he whom such weird terrors most appal;
Since these are fallow deer, and yonder dreams
   The dom'd Stuart Hospital,—

Was it the bugle echoing as of yore
   In some vast chase, enwrapt in lake-side mists ?
Swept Herne the Hunter by, or score on score
   Of silken Royalists ?

Hunts captured Charles? or hath Cromwellian shot
 Laid some escaping war-spent gallant low
In the far ride, where last year's leaf doth rot,
 And, save the deer, none go?

Who knows what stirs them? Nay, can any guess
 That which their beautiful clear eyes import
When, at high noon, about your hand they press,
 Begging in timid sort,

Save haply the exile's doom, which is the same
 Whether 'tis buried in the tragic eyes
Of king discrowned, or wanderer without name,
 Bondman, or brute that dies?

VICTOR PLARR.

NON SUM QUALIS ERAM BONAE SUB
REGNO CYNARAE

LAST night, ah, yesternight, betwixt her lips and mine
There fell thy shadow, Cynara ! thy breath was shed
Upon my soul, between the kisses and the wine;
And I was desolate and sick of an old passion,
   Yea ! I grew desolate and bowed my head;
I have been faithful to thee, Cynara ! in my fashion.

All night upon my breast I felt her warm heart beat;
Night-long within mine arms in love and sleep she lay;
Surely the kisses of her bought, red mouth were sweet
But I was desolate and sick of an old passion,
   When I awoke, and found the dawn was grey:
I have been faithful to thee, Cynara ! in my fashion.

I have forgot much, Cynara ! gone with the wind;
Flung roses, roses riotously with the throng;
Dancing to put thy pale, lost lilies out of mind;
But I was desolate, and sick of an old passion,
   Yea ! all the time because the dance was long !
I have been faithful to thee, Cynara ! in my fashion.

cried for madder music, and for stronger wine;
But when the feast is finished, and the lamps expire,
Then falls thy shadow, Cynara ! the night is thine;
And I am desolate and sick of an old passion,
   Yea ! hungry for the lips of my desire :—
have been faithful to thee, Cynara ! in my fashion !

ERNEST DOWSON.

EUTHANASIA

(Fin de siècle)

YES, this rich death were best :
Lay poison on thy lips, kiss me to sleep,
Or on the siren billow of thy breast
    Bring some voluptuous Lethe for life's pain,
        Some languorous nepenthe that will creep
           Drowsily from vein to vein;
        That slowly, drowsily, will steep
    Sense after sense, till, down long gulfs of rest
        Whirled like a leaf, I sink to the lone deep.

    It shall be afternoon,
And roses, roses breathing in the air !
Deliciously the splendour of deep June,
    Tempered through amber draperies, round us fall;
        And, like a dream of Titian, let thy hair
           Bosom and arms glow all,
        Clouds of love's sunset, o'er me there :
    Kiss that last kiss; then low some golden tune
        Sing, for the dirge of our superb despair.

So let the clock tick on,
Measuring the soft pulsations of Time's wing,
While to the pulseless ocean, like a swan
Abandoned to an unrelenting stream,
Floating, I hear thee faint and fainter sing;
Till death athwart my dream
Shall glide, robed like a Magian king,
And ease with poppies of oblivion
This heart, the scorpion Life no more may sting.

JOHN TODHUNTER.

Violets full, and the wild birds' song,
  Where the leaves grow green;
Where wind-flowers blow, and the blackbirds throng
  In their haunts unseen;
   Where the primroses peep,
    Here let me lie,
    Let me lie,
   Till I drink, in my sleep,
  A memory of flowers
  From the unforgotten hours,
And the perfume of the days gone by.

Violets closed, and the wild birds hushed,
  Where the dead leaves fall!
O the days when our sunrise flushed
  Red rays over all!

Where the brown owls peep,
    Here let me lie,
    Let me lie,
Where the years fell asleep,
Let me mourn for the flowers
Of the unforgotten hours,
And the perfume of the days gone by.

G. A. GREENE.

E

THE SECOND CRUCIFIXION

Loud mockers in the roaring street
  Say Christ is crucified again,
Twice pierced His Gospel-bringing feet,
  Twice broken His great heart in vain.

I hear, and to myself I smile,
For Christ talks with me all the while.

No angel now to roll the stone
  From off His unawaking sleep,
In vain shall Mary watch alone,
  In vain the soldiers vigil keep.

Yet, while they deem my Lord is dead,
My eyes are on His shining head.

Ah! never more shall Mary hear
  That voice exceeding sweet and low
Within the garden calling clear,
  Her Lord is gone, and she must go.

Yet all the while my Lord I meet
In every London lane and street.

Poor Lazarus shall wait in vain,
   And Bartimæus still go blind;
The healing hem shall ne'er again
   Be touched by suffering humankind.

Yet all the while I see them rest,
The poor and outcast, in His breast.

No more unto the stubborn heart
   With gentle knocking shall He plead,
No more the mystic pity start,
   For Christ twice dead is dead indeed.

So in the street I hear men say,
Yet Christ is with me all the day.

RICHARD LE GALLIENNE.

THE FIDDLER OF DOONEY

WHEN I play on my fiddle in Dooney,
  Folk dance like a wave of the sea.
My brother is priest in Kilvarnet,
  My cousin in Rossnaree.

I passed my brother and cousin,
  They read in a book of prayer;
I read in a book of songs
  I bought at the Sligo Fair.

When we come, at the close of Time,
  To Peter sitting in state,
He will smile on the three old spirits,
  But call me first through the gate.

For the good are always the merry,
  Save by an evil chance,
And the merry love the fiddle,
  And the merry love to dance.

And when the folk there spy me,
  They will all come up to me,
With 'Here is the fiddler of Dooney!'
  And dance like a wave of the sea.

W. B. YEATS.

ORPHEUS IN COVENT GARDEN

Down from the cliffs that rise sheer out of hell
He gazed awhile as one that masters doubt:
Then o'er the dark ravine the golden spell
Of clear-struck lyre and thrilling voice rang out.

As oft amid the Thracian hills of yore
The pard grew tame and fawned about his feet,
So they that wandered by that dolorous shore
Hung tranced upon that voice divinely sweet.

Around the charmer in the Indian land
The snakes cease not to sway their cunning heads,
And flap their dusky coils upon the sand
The while his reed a sleepy music sheds.

So that clear harp that clashed through all its strings
Soothed those within the gate of triple brass,
Until they mused upon forgotten things
Seen faintly as the shadows in a glass.

For us once more the antique lyre is strung
That gave the lost Eurydice release,
Since one whose birthright is the perfect tongue
Of Italy brings back the art of Greece.

ARTHUR CECIL HILLIER.

SONG IN THE LABOUR MOVEMENT

THE voice of labour soundeth shrill,
   Mere clamour of a tuneless throng,
To you who barter at your will
   The very life that maketh song.

Oh, you whose sluggard hours are spent
   The rule of Mammon to prolong,
What know you of the stern intent
   Of hosted labour marching strong?

When we have righted what is wrong
   Great singing shall your ears entreat;
Meanwhile in movement there is song,
   And music in the pulse of feet.

ERNEST RADFORD.

EVENING

(*Evensong*)

In the heart of a Saxon forest I followed the winding
ways
Deep cushioned with moss and barred with the sun-
set's slanting rays.

When out of the distance dim, where no end to the
path was seen,
But the breath of the Springtime hung like a motion-
less mist of green,

I heard a sound of singing, unearthly sad and clear,
Rise from the forest deeps and float on the evening
air.

I stopped and wondered and waited as it nearer and
nearer grew,
Louder and still more loud, till at last came into view—

No vision of spirits told of in weird old forest lore
Who roam the greenwood singing for ever and ever
    more—

But six Teutonic maidens tanned with the rain an
    sun,
A burthen of billetted wood on the shoulders of ever
    one.

How sturdily by they marched! and the chanting
    passed away
In the fragrant depths of the forest, and died with th
    dying day.

No spirits indeed—yet I thought, as awhile in dream
    I stood,
That a music more than earthly had passed through
    the darkening wood.

And I thought that the day to the morrow bequeathe
    in that solemn strain
The whole world's hope and labour, its love and it
    ancient pain.

T. W. ROLLESTON.

PEACE

Poor Peace, long silent in the market-place
  Stood sadly like a slave, where none would buy her ;
Yet now and then, there moved upon her face
  A mother's smile whose children tire and try her,
And now and then she looked within her veil
That bound her breast and throat and forehead pale.

But while she bent within the silent folding
  Where looped and swayed the veil beneath her breast,
It seemed some secret she was given for holding,
  Some secret like a little child at rest,
And now with less of patient grief she smiled ;
She had much solace from the sleeping child.

The market roared and rang all day around her :
  The buyer told his ever-new contempt,
The seller praised himself, but no one found her—
  From all the discord and the strife exempt,
Till night came softly, and the moon rose pale,
The mad world slept, and Peace unbound her veil.

And then, as when deep organ-music rolls
  One sound is lifted on a thousand prayers,
The child came forth, one form, a thousand souls,
  And now, from house to house, up quiet stairs
The gentle feet of his meek nurse neglected
Bore him, by men's oblivion less rejected.

And stepping softly to each fool forgetful
  Peace gave them back their souls for silent keeping;
But some she saw, and turned away, regretful,
  She could not trust their souls to them in sleeping,
And some, the teller of the old tale said,
She will but partly trust when they are dead.

EDWIN J. ELLIS.

SONG

WHAT are lips, but to be kissed?
  What are eyes, but to be praised?
What the fineness of a wrist?
  What the slimness of a waist?
What the softness of her hair,
If not that Love be tangled there?

What are lips, not to be kissed?
  What are eyes, not to be praised?
What is she, that would resist
  Love's desire to be embraced?
What her heart that will not dare
Suffer poor Love to linger there?

These are lips, fond to be kissed,
  These are eyes, fain to be praised:
And I think, if Love has missed
  Shelter in the wintry waste,
That this heart may soon prepare
Some nook for him to nestle there.

ARTHUR SYMONS.

DEATH AND THE PLAYER

I WATCHED the players playing on their stage;
    An old delightful comedy was theirs,
The very picture of a gallant age,
        Full of majestic airs.

Wit, virtuoso, captain, stately lord,—
    Each played his part with smooth Augustan grace,
And, grey and curled, th' Olympian perruques soared
        O'er each fine oval face.

Anon, young Celia, poised on high red heels,
    Advanced with Chloe, the discreet soubrette:
Her laughter rings abroad in silver peals;
        Her courtiers fawn and fret.

One was a whiskered son of awful Mars;
    And one, the favourite, a thing of spleen,
Whose pasquil jests, a stream of falling stars,
        Illumined all the scene.

They trod a minuet, and evermore,
   Betwixt the curtseying lady and her thrall,
A masked and shrouded dancer kept the floor,
      Unnoted by them all.

Alas, poor player, that was Death's Dance indeed !
   The curtain fell ; the masker's fleshless hand
Compelled thee to his chariot, which with speed
      Rolled home to his own land.

And now with cheeks and eyelids that confess
   Grim stains of the last midnight's gay disguise,
Th' ingenious haggard actors swiftly press
      Where their dead brother lies.

How strange a graveside—oh, how strange a scene !
   The player's double life in such eclipse !
What a morality would this have been
      On those once mocking lips !

But they are dumb, and there's scarce time for tears.
   Back to the town ! They're clamouring for our plays.
Tis good that arch-comedian Death appears
      But once in many days !

VICTOR PLARR.

IN OPERA-LAND

WHERE almond blossoms shed their snow
From garden walls of grey old Spain,
The Tritons of the fountain blow
Columns that break in diamond rain;
And 'neath the stars Elvira's voice
Bewails her fate in accents bland
Unto the gallant of her choice,
As is the mode in Opera-land.

Zerlina loosens her dark hair
And sings a snatch before the glass,
And brigands flirt with ladies fair
Who yield unto their charms, alas!
Their lords have pockets stuffed with gold
And boast their treasure to the band;
We know that way they have of old,
For it is mode in Opera-land.

In this last refuge of romance
Crusaders yet may hold their own,
And wandering gipsy girls may dance
Where camps are pitched and trumpets blown,
And soldiers dice upon the drums,
And pennons on the tents are fanned
By every wayward breeze that comes,
Such breeze as blows through Opera-land.

Assassins enter tightly masked,
And peasants trip it on the sod,
And guests arrive at balls unasked,
And statues in the churchyard nod,
And heroines march on serene
Through corpses strewn on either hand,
Nor ever show surprise, I ween;
It is not mode in Opera-land.

When these are laid upon the shelf,
Some Ibsenitish lady free
Her duty to her sex and self
May vaunt upon the natural B:
When moonlight and romance are dimmed
And old-world shrines no longer stand,
Ye gods! what will be preached and hymned
Within the realms of Opera-land!

F

Bold gipsy girls whose love is light,
And hermits of the desert sand,
Long be it ere your charms are trite
And ways are changed in Opera-land.

ARTHUR CECIL HILLIER.

GROWTH

I WATCHED the glory of her childhood change,
Half-sorrowful to find the child I knew,
   (Loved long ago in lily-time)
Become a maid, mysterious and strange,
With fair, pure eyes—dear eyes, but not the eyes I knew
     Of old, in the olden time !

Till on my doubting soul the ancient good
Of her dear childhood in the new disguise
   Dawned, and I hastened to adore
The glory of her waking maidenhood,
And found the old tenderness within her deepening eyes,
     But kinder than before.

ERNEST DOWSON.

QUATRAINS

Conscience (the Obverse)

CONSCIENCE is that fine critic of each thrill
   Along the spirit's nerves, with instinct sane
   For life's fine art assaying joy and pain,
His loves and hates canons of good and ill.

Conscience (the Reverse)

Conscience is but a child who fears the rod
Laid on by Mrs Grundy or by God ;
   But whose the stroke, or why they smite or spare
The smarting child scarce guesses.   That is odd !

JOHN TODHUNTER.

The Arch Magician

Art thou a man? Within thy mind's high hall
A magic mirror hangs upon the wall
   From out whose crystal dim the Magian, Thought,
Summons the shapes that ravish and appal.

JOHN TODHUNTER.

The New Sinai

Women were poets once, and dumbly wrought
Sweet love-songs from the perilous stuff of Thought,
   Now they have learnt to speak in dreadful prose,
Thundering in our dazed ears their *must* and *ought*.

JOHN TODHUNTER.

Creation

Behind me lay life's endless avatars,
  Before me vague unfathomable dread,
  In wastes of space where Death himself was dead :
Then God went by me, silent, sowing stars.

JOHN TODHUNTER.

The Golden Key

To love the right things rightly : this enspheres
  Wisdom, religion, art ; forges the key
That opens Eden through the Gate of Tears,
  Where by life's river blooms the mystic Tree.

JOHN TODHUNTER.

THE DARK ANGEL

Dark Angel, with thine aching lust
To rid the world of penitence:
Malicious Angel, who still dost
My soul such subtile violence !

Because of thee, no thought, no thing,
Abides for me undesecrate :
Dark Angel, ever on the wing,
Who never reachest me too late !

When music sounds, then changest thou
Its silvery to a sultry fire :
Nor will thine envious heart allow
Delight untortured by desire.

Through thee, the gracious Muses turn
To Furies, O mine Enemy !
And all the things of beauty burn
With flames of evil ecstasy.

Because of thee, the land of dreams
Becomes a gathering place of fears;
Until tormented slumber seems
One vehemence of useless tears.

When sunlight glows upon the flowers,
Or ripples down the dancing sea:
Thou, with thy troop of passionate powers,
Beleaguerest, bewilderest me.

Within the breath of autumn woods,
Within the winter silences:
Thy venomous spirit stirs and broods,
O master of impieties!

The ardour of red flame is thine,
And thine the steely soul of ice:
Thou poisonest the fair design
Of nature, with unfair device.

Apples of ashes, golden bright;
Waters of bitterness, how sweet:
O banquet of a foul delight,
Prepared by thee, dark Paraclete!

Thou art the whisper in the gloom,
The hinting tone, the haunting laugh:
Thou art the adorner of my tomb,
The minstrel of mine epitaph.

I fight thee, in the Holy Name!
Yet, what thou dost, is what God saith:
Tempter! should I escape thy flame,
Thou wilt have helped my soul from death:

The second death, that never dies,
That cannot die, when time is dead:
Live death, wherefrom the lost soul cries,
Eternally uncomforted.

Dark Angel, with thine aching lust!
Of two defeats, of two despairs:
Less dread, a change to drifting dust,
Than thine eternity of cares.

Do what thou wilt, thou shalt not so,
Dark Angel! triumph over me:
Lonely, unto the Lone I go;
Divine, to the Divinity.

LIONEL JOHNSON.

A MOOD

'They have taken away my Lord, and I know not where they have laid him.'

THEY have taken away my Lord;
   They have shattered the one great Hope;
   They have left us alone to cope
With our terrible selves : the sword

They broke, which the world restored;
   They have cast down the King from on high;
   Their derision has scaled the sky;
They have taken away my Lord.

The strength of immortal Love;
   The comfort of millions that weep;
   Prayer, and the Cross we adored—
All is lost ! there is no one above :
   We are left like the beasts that creep :
   They have taken away our Lord.

G. A. GREENE.

A MYSTICAL PRAYER TO THE MASTERS OF THE ELEMENTS, FINVARRA, FEACRA, AND CAOLTE

THE Powers, not kind like you, came where God's
       garden blows,
    And stole the crimson Rose,
And hurled it from its place amid the pearly light
    Into the blinding night,—
O, when shall Sorrow wander no more in the land
    With Beauty hand in hand?

Great elemental Powers of wind, and wave, and fire,
    With your harmonious quire,
Encircle her I love and sing her into peace,
    That my old care may cease,
And she forget the wandering and the crimson gloom
    Of the Rose in its doom.

Great Rulers of stillness, let her no longer be
   As the light on the sea,
Or as the changing spears flung by the golden stars
   Out of their whirling cars,
But let a gentle silence enwrought with music flow
   Where her soft footsteps go.

        W. B. YEATS.

HESPERIDES

MEN say—beyond the Western seas
   The happy isles no longer glow,
No sailor sights Hesperides,
   All that was long ago.

No longer in a glittering morn
   Their misty meadows flicker nigh,
No singing with the spray is borne,
   All that is long gone by.

To-day upon the golden beach
   No gold-haired guardian maidens stand,
No apples ripen out of reach,
   And none are mad to land.

The merchant-men, 'tis they say so,
   That trade across the Western seas,
In hurried transit to and fro,
   About Hesperides.

But, Reader, not as these thou art,
   So loose thy shallop from its hold,
And, trusting to the ancient chart,
   Thou'lt make them as of old.

RICHARD LE GALLIENNE.

ACKNOWLEDGMENT

Addressed to H.E.T.

FAIR flowers! the hand I fain would kiss
That so among you lightly moved,
To gather this—and this—and this—
The—while you nodded and approved.

In culling leaves so rare of scent,
It was—was it not—her intent
To grace a friendship old as ours
With fragrance passing that of flowers?

ERNEST RADFORD.

NIGHT

(After all)

WHEN the time comes for me to die,
  To-morrow, or some other day,
If God should bid me make reply,
  ' What would'st thou ? ' I shall say,

O God, Thy world was great and fair;
  Yet give me to forget it clean !
Vex me no more with things that were,
  And things that might have been.

I loved, I toiled, throve ill or well,
  —Lived certain years and murmured not.
Now grant me in that land to dwell
  Where all things are forgot.

For others, Lord, Thy purging fires,
  The loves reknit, the crown, the palm.
For me, the death of all desires
  In deep, eternal calm.

T. W. ROLLESTON.

SAINT ANTHONY

ALAS, poor Saint, you saw her too—
　　The white white bird, our spirits' lure.
Ah, then at last, at first you knew
　　How fair is fair, how pure is pure.
Why did she tempt your heaven-bound sense?
What devil had she?
　　　　　Her innocence.

And when you turned with laughter loud,
　　Though inward filled with hurrying fears,
Because your promised life was proud,
　　Nor might she know your fount of tears,
What angel moved with reverence
Your secret prayer?
　　　　　Her innocence.

EDWIN J. ELLIS.

A VARIATION UPON LOVE

FOR God's sake let me love you, and give over
These tedious protestations of a lover;
We're of one mind to love, and there's no let :
Remember that, and all the rest forget.
And let's be happy, mistress, while we may,
Ere yet to-morrow shall be called to-day.
To-morrow may be heedless, idle-hearted :
One night's enough for love to have met and parted
Then be it now, and I'll not say that I
In many several deaths for you would die ;
And I'll not ask you to declare that you
Will longer love than women mostly do
Leave words to them whom words, not doings, move
And let our silence answer for our love.

ARTHUR SYMONS.

A SECRET OF THE SEA

Down at the bottom of the sea,
    The huge old galleon lies asleep;
Red seaweeds cloak her heavily,
    Green seaweeds round her droop and sweep.

Scarce any light descends to show
    Her decks made black with ancient blood,
Or the few bones that dimly glow
    Where her stout captain last withstood

The drunken shock of his wild crew,
    Who welcomed freedom in his fall
With laughter, cursing, tears, and who
    Met with such shipwreck after all !

'Tis years since the faint noontide beam,
    That filters to the chart-room floor,
Last rested where, as in a dream,
    The drowned chief mutineer would pore

With orbits void and bony hands
  Upon the chart, which, day by day,
Into new shapes of seas and lands
  The exploring sea-worms fret and fray—

Years since that semblance of a man,
  That relic of unknown despair,
That symbol of past crime, began
  Obscurely to be no more there !

For centuries now the ship hath lain
  Down at the bottom of the sea,
Unknown, alone, save for some train
  Of shy small fishes starting by,

And so she still must lie until
  A dying sun be burning red,
And earthquakes all earth's caverns thrill,
  And the deep sea give up its dead !

                              VICTOR PLARR.

IN AN OLD LIBRARY

HERE the still air
Broods over drowsy nooks
Of ancient learning: one is ware,
  As in a mystic aisle
Of lingering incense, of the balm of books.
 So nard from cerecloths of Egyptian kings
  Solemnised once the sepulchres of Nile.

 Here quietness,
 A ghostly presence, dwells
Among rich tombs; here doth possess
  With an ecstatic dread
The intruder seeking old-world oracles
 In books, centuries of books, centuries of tombs
  That hold the spirits of the crownèd dead.

 Go softly ! Here
 Sleep fair embalmèd souls
In piled-up monuments, in their sere

And blazoned robes of fame,
Conquerors of Time.   Whisper to these grey scrolls,
Call Poet, Sage, Romancer, Chronicler,
And every one will answer to his name.

Man walks the earth,
The quintessence of dust :
Books from the ashes of his mirth,
Madness, and sorrow, seem
To draw the elixir of some rarer gust,
Or, like the stone of Alchemy, transmute
Life's cheating dross to golden truth of dream.

JOHN TODHUNTER.

THE GARDEN OF SHADOW

Love heeds no more the sighing of the wind
Against the perfect flowers : thy garden's close
Is grown a wilderness, where none shall find
One strayed, last petal of one last year's rose.

O bright, bright hair ! O mouth like a ripe fruit !
Can famine be so nigh to harvesting ?
Love that was songful, with a broken lute
In grass of graveyards goeth murmuring.

Let the wind blow against the perfect flowers,
And all thy garden change and glow with spring :
Love is grown blind ; with no more count of hours,
Nor part in seed-time nor in harvesting.

ERNEST DOWSON.

THE MEMORIAL GARDEN

HALF-SATED with the petalled chalice fair,
      Yet thieving still,
A roaming bee hums through the hot sweet air
      To poise at will.

Behind the speckled laurel and dark box,
      On either hand,
Crimson and golden-bright the hollyhocks
      Like sentries stand.

And here, 'neath sweeping boughs, and shadow flung
      And murm'rous sound,
A slender couch of twisted meshes hung
      Just o'er the ground.

Within the swaying net-work thou wouldst lie
      In ease serene :
Only a dome of leafy boughs on high,
      With sky between.

Dear, thou hast found amid the happy dead
        Shadow and rest;
And deeply sweet forgetfulness is shed
        Upon thy breast.

For us the cares that vex, the footsteps sore,
        The daily round,
For thee the stillness of the poppied shore
        And sleep profound.

The fretful changes of the day renew
        Their tedious flight,
Thine are the silences, the starry dew,
        The tides of night.

Thine are the mysteries that darkness yields
        To souls divine,
And the faint sweetnesses of dreaming fields
        And flowers are thine.

                        ARTHUR CECIL HILLIER.

THE CAP AND BELLS

A QUEEN was beloved by a jester,
   And once when the owls grew still
He made his soul go upward
   And stand on her window sill.

In a long and straight blue garment,
   It talked before morn was white,
And it had grown wise by thinking
   Of a footfall hushed and light.

But the young queen would not listen;
   She rose in her pale night gown,
She drew in the brightening casement
   And pushed the brass bolt down.

He bade his heart go to her,
   When the bats cried out no more,
In a red and quivering garment
   It sang to her through the door,

The tongue of it sweet with dreaming
   Of a flutter of flower-like hair,
But she took up her fan from the table
   And waved it off on the air.

'I've cap and bell,' he pondered,
   'I will send them to her and die.'
And as soon as the morn had whitened
   He left them where she went by.

She laid them upon her bosom,
   Under a cloud of her hair,
And her red lips sang them a love song.
   The stars grew out of the air.

She opened her door and her window,
   And the heart and the soul came through,
To her right hand came the red one,
   To her left hand came the blue.

They set up a noise like crickets,
   A chattering wise and sweet,
And her hair was a folded flower,
   And the quiet of love in her feet.

                    W. B. YEATS.

THE COMING OF WAR

GATHER the people, for the battle breaks :
    From camping grounds above the valley,
Gather the men at arms, and bid them rally;
    Because the morn, the battle, wakes.
High throned above the mountains and the main,
Triumphs the sun ! far down, the pasture plain
        To trampling armour shakes.

This was the meaning of those plenteous years,
    Those unarmed years of peace unbroken :
Flashing war crowns them ! Now war's trump hath
      spoken
    Their final glory in our ears.
The old blood of our pastoral fathers now
Riots about our heart, and through our brow :
        Their sons can have no fears.

This was our whispering and haunting dream,
    When cornlands flourished, red and golden;
When vines hung purple, nor could be withholden
    The radiant outburst of their stream.
Earth cried to us, that all her laboured store
Was ours : that she had more to give, and more :
       For nothing, did we deem ?

We give her back the glory of this hour.
    O sun and earth ! O strength and beauty !
We use you now, we thank you now : our duty
    We stand to do, mailed in your power.
A little people of a favoured land,
Helmed with the blessing of the morn we stand :
       Our life is at its flower.

Gather the people, let the battle break :
    An hundred peaceful years are over.
Now march each man to battle, as a lover :
    For him, whom death shall overtake,
Sleeping upon this field, about his gloom
Voices shall pierce, to thrill his sacred tomb,
       Of pride for his great sake.

With melody about us ; heart and feet
    Responding to one mighty measure:
Glad with the splendour of a sacred pleasure;

Swayed, one and all, as wind sways wheat :
Answering the sunlight with our eyes aglow,
Serene, and proud, and passionate, we go
        Through airs of morning sweet.

Let no man dare to be disheartened now !
        We challenge death beyond denial :
Against the host of death we make our trial :
        Lord God of Hosts ! do thou,
Who gavest us the fulness of thy sun
On fields of peace, perfect war's work begun :
        Warriors, to thee we bow.

O life-blood of remembrance !   Long ago
        This land upheld our ancient fathers :
And for this land, their land, our land, now gathers
        One fellowship against the foe.
The spears flash : be they as our mothers' eyes !
The trump sounds : hearken to our fathers' cries !
        March we to battle so.

LIONEL JOHNSON.

LADY MACBETH

(For a Picture by John S. Sargent, A.R.A.)

O LET me plant my feet upon the ground
　More firmly; stand erect and meet the sway
　And surge of royal Fate, before it stay.
This is the poise of Time, whence what rebound
I know not; for within this golden round
　I hold above my hair, those splendours play
　Which, be they for an age or for a day,
Shall blaze or burn upon my forehead crowned.

Why pause, O Queen foredestined? 'tis the way
　To mar e'en Fate, untaken on the bound—
　Lives there from that dread night some shadow of
　　　sound
Within mine ear? or from some future fray
　The clash of arms, disaster's disarray?
　Or is't the drip of blood upon the ground?

G. A. GREENE.

H

TIME'S MONOTONE

AUTUMN and Winter,
Summer and Spring—
Hath time no other song to sing?
Weary we grow of the changeless tune—
June and December,
December and June!

Time, like a bird, hath but one song,
One way to build, like a bird, hath he;
Thus hath he built so long, so long,
Thus hath he sung—ah me!

Time, like a spider, knows, be sure,
One only wile, though he seems so wise:
Death is his web, and Love his lure,
And you and I his flies.

'Love!' he sings
In the morning clear,
'Love! Love! Love!'
And you never hear

How under his breath
He whispers 'Death !
Death ! Death !'

Yet Time—'tis the strangest thing of all—
  Knoweth not the sense of the words he saith,
Eternity taught him his parrot-call
  Of 'Love and Death.'

Year after year doth the old man climb
  The mountainous knees of Eternity,
But Eternity telleth nothing to Time—
  It may not be.

RICHARD LE GALLIENNE.

THE SHELLEY MEMORIAL

(The Master's Speech).

'THE Rebel of eighty years ago
    Is the Hero of to-day.'
In this memorial none will know
The Rebel of eighty years ago.
We Oxford Dons, however slow,
   Are now at last compelled to say
'The Rebel of eighty years ago
    Is the Hero of to-day.'

ERNEST RADFORD.

THE WAIL OF THE DECADENT

    OH Heart of Man !
What ills torment, what passions tear
    The heart of man !
The Muses gathered in a clan
All, all with sad consent, declare
The burden is too hard to bear,
    Oh Heart of Man !

ERNEST RADFORD.

THE OLD SHEPHERD

THE old, old, shepherd scarcely heeds,
  Crouched on his thin old hams;
Making a small red fire of reeds
  He turns his back on the lambs.

'My old, old shepherd, now beware,
  My young, young lambs will stray,
Where is your pipe, your pastoral air,
  Your songs, and your crook to-day?'

'My pipe is here, it warms my hands,
  No need of songs, or crooks.
I know the meadows, cliffs, and sands,
  I know the ponds and brooks.

'I only fear to need no fears,—
  Sheep go the old, old way.
I would give half my few cold years
  Just to see one lamb stray.'

At night returned with peaceful mind,
  'Here are your flocks,' he said,
But the wolf had smelt that his eyes were blind,
  The crow, that my sheep were dead.

EDWIN J. ELLIS.

MIDSUMMER DAY

PALE, pure and lucent, o'er the quiet fields
  The purple twilight with its one white star
  Melts to the very heart of heaven afar,
And hardly to the summer darkness yields.

The dim white road like something ghostly leads
  Through trees that plead the majesty of time,
  And heard, I doubt not, in their leafy prime,
Of green Savannah-worlds and Raleigh's deeds.

In this deep quietude all things are blest
  Through tender dimness of the earth and sky :
  Save for a swallow's melancholy cry
All things at last are still and all have rest.

And yet beneath this twilight soft and bland
  The labyrinthine ways of London spread :
  The streets a million weary footsteps tread
From suburb brickfields to the roaring Strand.

ARTHUR CECIL HILLIER.

Ah, dans ces mornes séjours
Les jamais sont les toujours.

Paul Verlaine.

You would have understood me, had you waited;
    I could have loved you, dear! as well as he:
Had we not been impatient, dear! and fated
      Always to disagree.

What is the use of speech?   Silence were fitter:
    Lest we should still be wishing things unsaid.
Though all the words we ever spake were bitter,
      Shall I reproach you dead?

Nay, let this earth, your portion, likewise cover
    All the old anger, setting us apart:
Always, in all, in truth was I your lover;
      Always, I held your heart.

I have met other women who were tender,
    As you were cold, dear! with a grace as rare.
Think you, I turned to them, or made surrender,
      I who had found you fair?

Had we been patient, dear! ah, had you waited,
    I had fought death for you, better than he:
But from the very first, dear! we were fated
       Always to disagree.

Late, late, I come to you, now death discloses
    Love that in life was not to be our part:
On your low lying mound between the roses,
       Sadly I cast my heart.

I would not waken you: nay! this is fitter;
    Death and the darkness give you unto me;
Here we who loved so, were so cold and bitter,
       Hardly can disagree.

ERNEST DOWSON.

ON GREAT SUGARLOAF

WHERE Sugarloaf with bare and ruinous wedge
   Cleaves the grey air to view the darkening sea,
   We stood on high, and heard the northwind flee
Through clouds storm-heavy fallen from ledge to ledge.

Then sudden 'Look !' we cried.   The far black edge
   Of south horizon oped in sunbright glee,
   And a broad water shone, one moment free,
Ere darkness veiled again the wavering sedge.

Such is the Poet's inspiration, still
   Too evanescent ! coming but to go :
   Such the great passions shewing good in ill,

Quick brightnesses, love-lights too soon burnt low :
   And such Man's life, while flashes Heaven's will,
   Between two glooms a transitory glow.

G. A. GREENE.

CELTIC SPEECH

NEVER forgetful silence fall on thee,
   Nor younger voices overtake thee,
Nor echoes from thine ancient hills forsake thee,
   Old music heard by Mona of the Sea :
And where with moving melodies there break thee
   Pastoral Conway, venerable Dee.

Like music lives, nor may that music die,
   Still in the far, fair Gaelic places :
The speech, so wistful with its kindly graces,
   Holy Croagh Patrick knows, and holy Hy :
The speech, that wakes the soul in withered faces,
   And wakes remembrance of great things gone by.

Like music by the desolate Land's End,
   Mournful forgetfulness hath broken :
No more words kindred to the winds are spoken,
   Where upon iron cliffs whole seas expend
That strength, whereof the unalterable token
   Remains wild music, even to the world's end.

LIONEL JOHNSON.

THE NIGHT-JAR*

On the river, in the shallows, on the shore,
   Are the darkness and the silence of the tomb;
O'er the woods the sunset tinged an hour before
      Utter gloom.

'Twixt the ramparts of the mighty aspen trees,
   In midstream, the pallid waters gleam afar,
Not a ripple on their surface, not a breeze,
      Not a star.

Where the shadow of the ruined water-mill
   Hides the mill-pool and its anchored lily fleet,
And the warm air seems to slumber over-still,
      Over-sweet,

Hark the Night-jar !   In the meadows by the stream
   Sounds the bird's unearthly note : I like it well,
For it lulls you as the mystery of a dream,
      Or a spell.

* ' They are the witches among birds.'

All the nightingales along the bowery reach
   Plain together when the midnight moon is bright :
This bird only knows by heart the secret speech
        Of dark night.

Turn the boat now ! row away, friends ; let us hence,
   Lest the glamour of the night's o'er-trancing breath
Plunge us one and all into that dream intense
        Which is Death !

                  VICTOR PLARR.

THE SONG OF THE OLD MOTHER

I RISE in the dawn, and I kneel and blow
Till the seed of the fire flicker and glow.
And then I must scrub, and bake, and sweep,
Till stars are beginning to blink and peep,
But the young lie long and dream in their bed
Of the matching of ribbons, the blue and the red,
And their day goes over in idleness,
And they sigh if the wind but lift up a tress.
While I must work, because I am old
And the seed of the fire gets feeble and cold.

W. B. YEATS.

THE FIRST SPRING DAY

YES it is Spring's
First breath ! O the soft wind
That, ranging through my garden solitude
Upon his murmuring wings,
Wakes in all tender things
The bliss of life renewed !

Somewhere, I know,
The lark's wild ecstasy
Is shaking the blue sky,
Though winter's latest snow
In far-off crannies of the purple hill,
By noon untrodden, still
Lingering may lie.

For March, the churl, this one sweet day,
Smiles at my window from the South,
As though the virgin kiss of new-born May
Were warm upon his mouth.

He woos me to look out and see
　　How the bright sun
Sets budding every tree,
　　And wakes the flowers each one.
Crocuses peering up,
Joy in each golden cup,
　　Say : 'Winter's reign is done ! '
And in my orchard-close the sweet birds sing :
　　' No more Winter is king,
Open your windows, and let in the Spring ! '

JOHN TODHUNTER.

AN ODE TO SPRING

Is it the Spring?
  Or are the birds all wrong,
That play on flute and viol,
  A thousand strong,
In minstrel galleries
  Of the long deep wood,
Epiphanies
  Of bloom and bud.

Grave minstrels those,
  Of deep responsive chant;
But see how yonder goes,
  Dew-drunk, with giddy slant,
Yon Shelley-lark
  And hark !
Him on the giddy brink
  Of pearly Heaven
His fairy anvil clink

I

Or watch, in fancy,
    How the brimming note
Falls like a string of pearls
    From out his heavenly throat;
Or like a fountain
    In Hesperides,
Raining its silver rain,
    In gleam and chime,
On backs of ivory girls—
    Twice happy rhyme!—
Ah, none of these
    May make it plain,
No image we may seek
Shall match the magic of his gurgling beak.

And many a silly thing
    That hops and cheeps,
And perks his tiny tail,
    And sideway peeps,
And flutters little wing,
    Seems in his consequential way
To tell of Spring.

The river warbles soft and runs
    With fuller curve and sleeker line,
Though on the winter-blackened hedge
    Twigs of unbudding iron shine,
And trampled still the river-sedge.

And O the Sun!
I have no friend so generous as this Sun
That comes to meet me with his big warm hands.
And O the Sky!
There is no maid, how true,
Is half so chaste
As the pure kiss of greening willow wands
Against the intense pale blue
Of this sweet boundless over-arching waste.

And see!—dear Heaven, but it is the Spring!—
    See yonder, yonder, by the river there,
Long glittering pearly fingers flash
    Upon the warm bright air:
Why 'tis the heavenly palm,
    The Christian tree,
Whose budding is a psalm
    Of natural piety;
Soft silver notches up the smooth green stem,
    Ah, Spring must follow them,
It is the Spring!

O spirit of Spring,
    Whose strange instinctive art
Makes the bird sing,
    And brings the bud again;
O in my heart
    Take up thy heavenly reign,

And from its deeps
  Draw out the hidden flower,
And where it sleeps,
  Throughout the winter long,
O sweet mysterious power,
  Awake the slothful song!

RICHARD LE GALLIENNE.

A PRESIDING EXAMINER

EMERGING from the darkness
  Of London's sullen frown,
I simulating Majesty
  Appeared in hood and gown,

Commissioned to examine,
  According to the rule,
In all that they could cram in,
  The boys of my old school.

    *   *   *   *

I sat in my imposing seat:
  The papers from me flew
As though my learning were complete,
  And I all knowledge knew.

But O! despite the hood and gown,
  Despite the high respect
Paid to a mild official frown,
  Yet had I to reflect

That 'neath a borrowed mortar-board
　　Mere ghosts of knowledge dwelt;
That false was my pretended hoard :
　　Ah me, how poor I felt !

Ah boys, despite my college,
　　I am a learnèd man :
I've loads of sorry knowledge
　　Not set in any plan.

My wisdom hard in earning
　　I'd give it all to know
Again what I was learning
　　Now twenty years ago.

ERNEST RADFORD.

A RHYME ON RHYME

Who made first our words resemble
With division and with tremble,
Saving them from song's perdition
The abyss of repetition,
And gave the flower of rhyme from earth to air for air's
    fruition?

Did he measure all the meaning
Of the rhymes he left for gleaning
In the dancing hand and hand?
Did he know the joyous band?
Did he see the singing sisters, did he love and under-
    stand?

There was no such old Magician.
The blind murmurs of Tradition
Dimly shaped and never knew
Of those sounds so sweet and few
That make metre all one vessel and her singers all one
    crew.

Music pouring from the boundless
Sheds her life upon the soundless.
Pretty rhyme, while doves are cooing,
Looking down on lovers wooing,
Adds the sisterhood of saying to the brotherhood of
    doing.

EDWIN J. ELLIS.

List of Books
in
Belles Lettres

1894

Telegraphic Address—
'BODLEIAN, LONDON.'

'A WORD must be said for the manner in which the publishers have produced the volume (*i.e.*, "The Earth Fiend"), a sumptuous folio, printed by CONSTABLE, the etchings on Japanese paper by MR. GOULDING. The volume should add not only to MR. STRANG'S fame but to that of MESSRS. ELKIN MATHEWS AND JOHN LANE, who are rapidly gaining distinction for their beautiful editions of belles-lettres.'—*Daily Chronicle*, Sept. 24, 1892.

Referring to MR. LE GALLIENNE'S 'English Poems' *and* 'Silhouettes' by MR. ARTHUR SYMONS:—'We only refer to them now to note a fact which they illustrate, and which we have been observing of late, namely, the recovery to a certain extent of good taste in the matter of printing and binding books. These two books, which are turned out by MESSRS. ELKIN MATHEWS AND JOHN LANE, are models of artistic publishing, and yet they are simplicity itself. The books with their excellent printing and their very simplicity make a harmony which is satisfying to the artistic sense.'—*Sunday Sun*, Oct. 2, 1892.

'MR. LE GALLIENNE is a fortunate young gentleman. I don't know by what legerdemain he and his publishers work, but here, in an age as stony to poetry as the ages of Chatterton and Richard Savage, we find the full edition of his book sold before publication. How is it done, MESSRS. ELKIN MATHEWS AND JOHN LANE? for, without depreciating MR. LE GALLIENNE'S sweetness and charm, I doubt that the marvel would have been wrought under another publisher. These publishers, indeed, produce books so delightfully, that it must give an added pleasure to the hoarding of first editions.'—KATHARINE TYNAN in *The Irish Daily Independent*.

'To MESSRS. ELKIN MATHEWS AND JOHN LANE almost more than to any other, we take it, are the thanks of the grateful singer especially due; for it is they who have managed, by means of limited editions and charming workmanship, to impress book-buyers with the belief that a volume may have an æsthetic and commercial value. They have made it possible to speculate in the latest discovered poet, as in a new company—with the difference that an operation in the former can be done with three half-crowns.'—*St. James's Gazette*.

May, 1894.

List of Books

IN

BELLES LETTRES

(Including some Transfers)

PUBLISHED BY

Elkin Mathews & John Lane

The Bodley Head

VIGO STREET, LONDON, W.

◆§§§◆

ADAMS (FRANCIS).

ESSAYS IN MODERNITY. cr. 8vo. 5s. *net*.
[*In preparation.*

ALLEN (GRANT).

THE LOWER SLOPES: A VOLUME OF VERSE, with title page and cover design by J. ILLINGWORTH KAY. 600 copies, cr. 8vo. 5s. *net*.

ANTÆUS.

THE BACKSLIDER, AND OTHER POEMS. 100 only, sm. 4to. 7s. 6d. *net*. [*Very few remain.*

BENSON (EUGENE).

> FROM THE ASOLAN HILLS. A Poem. 300 copies, imp. 16mo. 5s. *net.* [*Very few remain.*

BINYON (LAURENCE).

> LYRIC POEMS, with title page by SELWYN IMAGE. Sq. 16mo. 5s. *net.*

BOURDILLON (F. W.).

> A LOST GOD. A Poem, with Illustrations by H. J. FORD. 500 copies, 8vo. 6s. *net.* [*Very few remain.*

CHAPMAN (ELIZABETH RACHEL).

> A LITTLE CHILD'S WREATH : A Sonnet Sequence. 350 copies. Sq. 16mo. 3s. 6d. *net.*

COLERIDGE (HON. STEPHEN).

> THE SANCTITY OF CONFESSION. A Romance. 2nd edition, cr. 8vo. 3s. *net.* [*A few remain.*

CRANE (WALTER).

> RENASCENCE. A Book of Verse. Frontispiece and 38 designs by the Author. [*Small paper edition out of print.* There remain a few large paper copies, fcap. 4to. £1. 1s. *net.* And a few fcap. 4to. Japanese vellum. £1. 15s. *net.*

CROSSING (WM.)

> THE ANCIENT CROSSES OF DARTMOOR. With 11 plates, 8vo. cloth. 4s. 6d. *net.* [*Very few remain.*

DAVIDSON (JOHN).

> PLAYS : An Unhistorical Pastoral ; A Romantic Farce ; Bruce, a Chronicle Play ; Smith, a Tragic Farce ; Scaramouch in Naxos, a Pantomime, with a frontispiece and cover design by AUBREY BEARDSLEY. 500 copies. Small 4to. 7s. 6d. *net.*

DAVIDSON (JOHN).

THE NORTH WALL. Fcap. 8vo. 2s. 6d. *net.* [*Very few remain. Transferred by the Author to the present Publishers.*

DAVIDSON (JOHN).

FLEET STREET ECLOGUES. 2nd edition, fcap. 8vo. buckram,
5s. net.

DAVIDSON (JOHN).

A RANDOM ITINERARY : Prose Sketches, with a Ballad.
Frontispiece, title page, and cover design by LAURENCE
HOUSMAN. 600 copies. Fcap. 8vo., Irish linen.
5s. net.

DE GRUCHY (AUGUSTA).

UNDER THE HAWTHORN, AND OTHER VERSES. *Frontis-
piece by Walter Crane.* 300 copies, cr. 8vo. 5s. net.
Also 30 copies on Japanese vellum. 15s. net.
[*Very few remain.*

DE TABLEY (LORD).

POEMS, DRAMATIC AND LYRICAL. By JOHN LEICESTER
WARREN (Lord De Tabley), illustrations and cover
design by C. S. RICKETTS. 2nd edition, cr. 8vo.
7s. 6d. net.

FIELD (MICHAEL).

SIGHT AND SONG (Poems on Pictures). 400 copies, fcap.
8vo. 5s. net.   [*Very few remain.*

FIELD (MICHAEL).

STEPHANIA : A TRIALOGUE IN 3 ACTS. 250 copies,
pott 4to. 6s. net.   [*Very few remain.*

GALE (NORMAN).

ORCHARD SONGS, with title page and cover design by
J. ILLINGWORTH KAY.   Fcap. 8vo., Irish linen.
5s. net.
Also a special edition, limited in number, on hand-made
paper, bound in English vellum. £1. 1s. net.

GARNETT (RICHARD).

POEMS, with title page designed by J. ILLINGWORTH KAY.
350 copies, cr. 8vo. 5s. net.

GOSSE (EDMUND).

THE LETTERS OF THOMAS LOVELL BEDDOES. Now
first edited. Pott 8vo. 5s. net.

GRAHAME (KENNETH).

PAGAN PAPERS: A VOLUME OF ESSAYS, with title page by AUBREY BEARDSLEY. Fcap. 8vo. 5s. net.

GREENE (G. A.).

ITALIAN LYRISTS OF TO-DAY. Translations in the original metres from about 35 living Italian poets ; with bibliographical and biographical notes, cr. 8vo. 5s. net.

HAKE (DR. T. GORDON).

A SELECTION FROM HIS POEMS. Edited by Mrs. MEYNELL, with a portrait after D. G. ROSSETTI, and a cover design by GLEESON WHITE. Cr. 8vo. 5s. net.

HALLAM (ARTHUR HENRY).

THE POEMS, together with his Essay "On some of the Characteristics of Modern Poetry and on the Lyrical Poems of Alfred Tennyson." Edited, with an introduction, by RICHARD LE GALLIENNE, 550 copies, fcap. 8vo. 5s. net.   [Very few remain.

HAMILTON (COL. IAN).

THE BALLAD OF HADJI, AND OTHER POEMS. Etched frontispiece by WM. STRANG. 550 copies, fcap. 8vo. 3s. net.

Transferred by the Author to the present Publishers.

HAZLITT (WILLIAM).

LIBER AMORIS: a reprint of the 1823 edition, with numerous original documents appended, never before printed, including MRS. HAZLITT's Diary in Scotland ; Portrait after BEWICK ; Facsimile Letters, &c. ; and the critical introduction by RICHARD LE GALLIENNE prefixed to the edition of 1893. 400 copies. 4to., green buckram. £1. 1s. net.   [Very shortly.

HICKEY (EMILY H.).

VERSE TALES, LYRICS, AND TRANSLATIONS. 300 copies, imp. 16mo. 5s. net.

HORNE (HERBERT P.).

DIVERSI COLORES. Poems with ornaments by the Author, 250 copies, 16mo. 5s. *net.*

JAMES (W. P.).

ROMANTIC PROFESSIONS : A VOLUME OF ESSAYS. With title page by J. ILLINGWORTH KAY. 450 copies. Cr. 8vo., buckram. 5s. *net.*

JOHNSON (EFFIE).

IN THE FIRE, AND OTHER FANCIES. Frontispiece by WALTER CRANE. 500 copies, imp. 16mo. 3s. 6d. *net.*

JOHNSON (LIONEL).

THE ART OF THOMAS HARDY. Six Essays, with etched portrait by WM. STRANG, and bibliography by JOHN LANE, cr. 8vo. 5s. 6d. *net.*
Also 150 copies, large paper, with proofs of the portrait.
£1. 1s. *net.*   [*Very Shortly.*

JOHNSON (LIONEL).

A VOLUME OF POEMS, fcap. 8vo. 5s. *net.* [*In preparation.*

KEATS (JOHN).

THREE ESSAYS, now issued in book form for the first time. Edited by H. BUXTON FORMAN, with life mask by HAYDON. Fcap. 4to. 10s. 6d. *net.* [*Very few remain.*

KEYNOTES SERIES.

Each Volume with specially-designed title page by AUBREY BEARDSLEY, cr. 8vo., cloth. 3s. 6d. *net.*

Vol.   I. KEYNOTES, by GEORGE EGERTON.
                            [*Fourth Edition now ready.*
Vol. II. THE DANCING FAUN, by FLORENCE FARR.
Vol. III. POOR FOLK. Translated from the Russian of F. DOSTOIEVSKY, by LENA MILMAN, with a preface by GEORGE MOORE.
Vol. IV. A CHILD OF THE AGE, by FRANCIS ADAMS.
                            [*In rapid preparation*
Vol.   V. THE GREAT GOD PAN AND THE INMOST LIGHT, by ARTHUR MACHEN.   [*In preparation.*

LEATHER (R. K.).

>   VERSES. 250 copies, fcap. 8vo.   3s. *net.*
>   *Transferred by the Author to the present Publishers.*

LEATHER (R. K.), & RICHARD LE GALLIENNE.

>   THE STUDENT AND THE BODY-SNATCHER, AND OTHER
>   TRIFLES.   [*Small paper edition out of print.*
>   There remain a very few of the 50 large paper copies.
>   7s. 6d. *net.*

LE GALLIENNE (RICHARD).

>   PROSE FANCIES, with a portrait of the Author, by WILSON
>   STEER.   Crown 8vo., purple cloth, uniform with
>   "THE RELIGION OF A LITERARY MAN."   5s. *net.*
>   Also a limited large paper edition.   8vo.   12s. 6d. *net.*
>   [*Immediately.*

LE GALLIENNE (RICHARD).

>   THE BOOK BILLS OF NARCISSUS.   An account rendered
>   by RICHARD LE GALLIENNE.   2nd edition, cr. 8vo.,
>   buckram.   3s. 6d. *net.*

LE GALLIENNE (RICHARD).

>   ENGLISH POEMS.   3rd edition, cr. 8vo., purple cloth,
>   uniform with "THE RELIGION OF A LITERARY
>   MAN."   5s. *net.*

LE GALLIENNE (RICHARD).

>   GEORGE MEREDITH : Some Characteristics ; with a Biblio-
>   graphy (much enlarged) by JOHN LANE, portrait, &c.
>   3rd edition, cr. 8vo.   5s. 6d. *net.*

LE GALLIENNE (RICHARD).

>   THE RELIGION OF A LITERARY MAN.   4th thousand.
>   Cr. 8vo., purple cloth.   3s. 6d. *net.*
>   Also a special rubricated edition on hand-made paper.
>   8vo.   10s. 6d. *net.*

LETTERS TO LIVING ARTISTS.

>   500 copies, fcap. 8vo.   3s. 6d. net.   [*Very few remain.*

MARSTON (PHILIP BOURKE).

A Last Harvest : Lyrics and Sonnets from the Book of Love. Edited by Louise Chandler Moulton. 500 copies, fcap. 8vo. 5s. net.
Also 50 copies on large paper, hand-made. 10s. 6d. net.
[Very few remain.

MARTIN (W. WILSEY).

Quatrains, Life's Mystery, and Other Poems. 16mo. 2s. 6d. net. [Very few remain.

MARZIALS (THEO.).

The Gallery of Pigeons, and Other Poems. Fcap. 8vo. 4s. 6d. net. [Very few remain.
Transferred by the Author to the present Publishers.

MEYNELL (MRS.) (ALICE C. THOMPSON).

Poems. 2nd edition, fcap. 8vo. 3s. 6d. net. A few of the 50 large paper copies (1st edition) remain. 12s. 6d. net.

MEYNELL (MRS.).

The Rhythm of Life, and Other Essays. 2nd Edition, fcap. 8vo. 3s. 6d. net. A few of the 50 large paper copies (1st edition) remain. 12s. 6d. net.

MONKHOUSE (ALLAN).

Books and Plays : a Volume of Essays. 400 copies. crown 8vo. 5s. net. [Immediately.

MURRAY (ALMA).

Portrait as Beatrice Cenci. With critical notice, containing four letters from Robert Browning. 8vo. wrapper. 2s. net.

NETTLESHIP (J. T.).

Robert Browning. Essays and Thoughts. Third edition, cr. 8vo. 5s. 6d. net. In preparation. Half a dozen of the Whatman L.P. copies (first edition) remain. £1. 1s. net.

NOBLE (JAS. ASHCROFT).

> THE SONNET IN ENGLAND, AND OTHER ESSAYS. Title-
> page and cover design by AUSTIN YOUNG. 600 copies.
> cr. 8vo. 5s. *net.*
> Also 50 copies L.P. 12s. 6d. *net.*

NOEL (HON. RODEN).

> POOR PEOPLE'S CHRISTMAS. 250 copies. 16mo. 1s. *net.*
> [*Very few remain.*

OXFORD CHARACTERS.

> A series of lithographed portraits by WILL ROTHENSTEIN,
> with text by F. YORK POWELL and others. To be
> issued monthly in term. Each part will contain two
> portraits. Parts I. to V. ready, 200 sets only, folio,
> wrapper. 5s. *net* per part. Also 25 special large paper
> sets, containing proofs of the portraits, signed by the
> artist. 10s. 6d. *net* per part.

PINKERTON (PERCY).

> GALEAZZO : a Venetian Episode, and other Poems. Etched
> frontispiece. 16mo. 5s. *net.*   [*Very few remain.*
> *Transferred by the Author to the present Publishers.*

RADFORD (DOLLIE).

> SONGS. A new volume of verse.   [*In preparation*

RADFORD (ERNEST).

> CHAMBERS TWAIN. Frontispiece by WALTER CRANE.
> 250 copies. Imp. 16mo. 5s. *net.*
> Also 50 copies large paper. 10s. 6d. *net.* [*Very few remain.*

RHYMERS' CLUB, THE SECOND BOOK OF THE.

> With contributions by E. DOWSON, E. J. ELLIS, G. A.
> GREENE, A. HILLIER, L. JOHNSON, R. LE GALLIENNE,
> V. PLARR, E. RADFORD, E. RHYS, T. W. ROLLESTON,
> A. SYMONS, J. TODHUNTER, and W. B. YEATS.
> 500 copies (400 for sale). Sq. 16mo. 5s. *net.* Also
> 50 copies large paper, 10s. 6d. *net.*   [*Immediately.*

RHYS (ERNEST).

A LONDON ROSE, AND OTHER RHYMES, with title page designed by SELWYN IMAGE. 350 copies, cr. 8vo., 5s. *net.*

RICKETTS (C. S.) and C. H. SHANNON.

HERO AND LEANDER. By CHRISTOPHER MARLOWE and GEORGE CHAPMAN, with borders, initials, and illustrations designed and engraved on the wood by C. S. RICKETTS and C. H. SHANNON. Bound in English vellum and gold. 200 copies only. 35s. *net.*

SCHAFF (DR. P.).

LITERATURE AND POETRY: Papers on Dante, etc. Portrait and Plates. 100 copies only. 8vo. 10s. *net.*

STODDARD (R. H.).

THE LION'S CUB : WITH OTHER VERSE. Portrait. 100 copies only, bound in an illuminated Persian design. Fcap. 8vo. 5s. *net.* [*Very few remain.*

STREET (G. S.).

THE AUTOBIOGRAPHY OF A BOY. Passages selected by his friend G. S. S., with title page designed by C. W. FURSE. 500 copies, fcap. 8vo. 3s. 6d. *net.*

SYMONDS (JOHN ADDINGTON).

IN THE KEY OF BLUE, AND OTHER PROSE ESSAYS. Cover design by C. S. RICKETTS. 2nd edition, thick cr. 8vo. 8s. 6d. *net.*

THOMPSON (FRANCIS).

A VOLUME OF POEMS. With frontispiece, title page, and cover design by LAURENCE HOUSMAN. 4th edition, pott 4to. 5s. *net.*

TODHUNTER (JOHN).

A SICILIAN IDYLL. Frontispiece by WALTER CRANE. 250 copies. Imp. 16mo. 5s. *net.*
Also 50 copies on hand-made large paper, fcap. 4to. 10s. 6d. *net.* [*Very few remain.*

TOMSON (GRAHAM R.).

> AFTER SUNSET. A volume of Poems. With title page and
> cover design by R. ANNING BELL. Fcap. 8vo. 5s. *net.*
> Also a limited large paper edition. 12s. 6d. *net.*
> > [*In preparation.*

TREE (H. BEERBOHM).

> THE IMAGINATIVE FACULTY. A Lecture delivered at the
> Royal Institution. With portrait of MR. TREE from
> an unpublished drawing by the MARCHIONESS OF
> GRANBY. Fcap. 8vo., boards. 2s. 6d. *net.*

TYNAN HINKSON (KATHARINE).

> CUCKOO SONGS. With title page and cover design by
> LAURENCE HOUSMAN. 500 copies, fcap. 8vo. 5s. *net.*

VAN DYKE (HENRY).

> THE POETRY OF TENNYSON. 3rd edition, enlarged, cr.
> 8vo. 5s. 6d. *net.*
>
> *The late Laureate himself gave valuable aid in correcting
> various details.*

WATSON (WILLIAM).

> THE ELOPING ANGELS : A CAPRICE. Second edition,
> sq. 16mo. buckram. 3s. 6d. *net.*

WATSON (WILLIAM).

> EXCURSIONS IN CRITICISM : BEING SOME PROSE RECREA-
> TIONS OF A RHYMER. 2nd edition, cr. 8vo. 5s. *net.*

WATSON (WILLIAM).

> THE PRINCE'S QUEST, AND OTHER POEMS. With a
> bibliographical note added. 2nd edition, fcap. 8vo.
> 4s. 6d. *net.*

WEDMORE (FREDERICK).

> PASTORALS OF FRANCE—RENUNCIATIONS. A volume of
> Stories. Title-page by JOHN FULLEYLOVE, R.I. 3rd
> edition, cr. 8vo. 5s. *net.*
>
> *A few of the large paper copies of Renunciations* (1st *Edition*)
> *remain.* 10s. 6d. *net.*

WICKSTEED (P. H.).

> DANTE : SIX SERMONS. 3rd edition, cr. 8vo. 2s. *net.*

WILDE (OSCAR).

> THE SPHINX. A poem decorated throughout in line and colour, and bound in a design by CHARLES RICKETTS. 250 copies.   £2. 2s. net.   25 copies large paper. £5. 5s. net.

WILDE (OSCAR).

> The incomparable and ingenious history of Mr. W. H., being the true secret of Shakespear's sonnets now for the first time here fully set forth, with initial letters and cover design by CHARLES RICKETTS. 500 copies. 10s. 6d. net.   Also 50 copies large paper.   21s. net.
> *[In preparation.*

WILDE (OSCAR).

> DRAMATIC WORKS, now printed for the first time with a specially designed binding to each volume by CHARLES SHANNON. 500 copies, sm. 4to.   7s. 6d. net per vol. Also 50 copies large paper.   15s. net per vol.
>
> Vol. I. LADY WINDERMERE'S FAN. A comedy in four acts.
> Vol. II. A WOMAN OF NO IMPORTANCE. A comedy in four acts.   [*Immediately.*
> Vol. III. THE DUCHESS OF PADUA. A blank verse tragedy in five acts.   [*Shortly.*

WILDE (OSCAR).

> SALOME. A Tragedy in one Act, done into English, with title page, 10 illustrations, tail piece, and cover design by AUBREY BEARDSLEY. 500 copies, sm. 4to.   15s. net. Also 100 copies large paper.   30s. net.

WYNNE (FRANCES).

> WHISPER. A volume of Verse. Fcap. 8vo.   2s. 6d. net. *Transferred by the Author to the present Publishers.*
>
> A Memoir by KATHARINE TYNAN, and a portrait, have been added.

The Hobby Horse

A new series of this illustrated magazine will be published quarterly by subscription, under the Editorship of HERBERT P. HORNE. Subscription £1 per annum, post free, for the four numbers. Quarto, printed on hand-made paper, and issued in a limited edition to subscribers only. The Magazine will contain articles upon Literature, Music, Painting, Sculpture, Architecture, and the Decorative Arts; Poems; Essays; Fiction; original Designs; with reproductions of pictures and drawings by the old masters and contemporary artists. There will be a new title-page and ornaments designed by the Editor. Among the contributors to the Hobby Horse are :

The late MATTHEW ARNOLD.
LAURENCE BINYON.
WILFRID BLUNT.
FORD MADOX BROWN.
The late ARTHUR BURGESS.
E. BURNE-JONES, A.R.A.
AUSTIN DOBSON.
RICHARD GARNETT, LL.D.
A. J. HIPKINS, F.S.A.
SELWYN IMAGE.
LIONEL JOHNSON.
RICHARD LE GALLIENNE.
SIR F. LEIGHTON, Bart., P.R.A.
T. HOPE MCLACHLAN.
MAY MORRIS.
C. HUBERT H. PARRY, Mus. Doc.
A. W. POLLARD.

F. YORK POWELL.
CHRISTINA G. ROSSETTI.
W. M. ROSSETTI.
JOHN RUSKIN, D.C.L., LL.D.
FREDERICK SANDYS.
The late W. BELL SCOTT.
FREDERICK J. SHIELDS.
J. H. SHORTHOUSE.
The late JAMES SMETHAM.
SIMEON SOLOMON.
A. SOMERVELL.
The late J. ADDINGTON SYMONDS.
KATHARINE TYNAN.
G. F. WATTS, R.A.
FREDERICK WEDMORE.
OSCAR WILDE.

Prospectuses on Application.

THE BODLEY HEAD, VIGO STREET, LONDON, W.

'Nearly every book put out by Messrs. Elkin Mathews and John Lane, at the Sign of the Bodley Head, is a satisfaction to the special senses of the modern bookman, for bindings, shapes, types, and papers. They have surpassed themselves, and registered a real achievement in English bookmaking by the volume of " Poems, Dramatic and Lyrical," of Lord De Tabley.'
Newcastle Daily Chronicle.

'A ray of hopefulness is stealing again into English poetry after the twilight greys of Clough, Arnold, and Tennyson. Even unbelief wears braver colours. Despite the jeremiads, which are the dirges of the elder gods, England is still a nest of singing-birds (*teste* the Catalogue of Elkin Mathews and John Lane).'—MR. ZANGWILL, in *Pall Mall Magazine.*

'One can nearly always be certain, when one sees on the title-page of any given book the name of Messrs. Elkin Mathews and John Lane as being the publishers thereof, that there will be something worth reading to be found between the boards.'—*World.*

'All Messrs. Mathews and Lane's books are so beautifully printed and so tastefully issued, that it rejoices the heart of a book-lover to handle them ; but they have shewn their sound judgment not less markedly in the literary quality of their publications. The choiceness of form is not inappropriate to the matter, which is always of something more than ephemeral worth. This was a distinction on which the better publishers at one time prided themselves ; they never lent their names to trash ; but some names associated with worthy traditions have proved more than once a delusion and a snare. The record of Messrs. Elkin Mathews and John Lane is perfect in this respect, and their imprint is a guarantee of the worth of what they publish.'—*Birmingham Daily Post, Nov. 6th,* 1893.